"In 2000 Perry Noble shared with me his dr[...] of one thousand people. As we talked, I sense[...] so it did not surprise me when I received a ca[...] know that the church had reached one thousand attendees. Much to my delight, I have received fifteen additional notes from Perry—every time another goal of one thousand is reached. Today as I write this, the average attendance of all seven campuses of NewSpring Church is sixteen thousand people. It has been my joy and delight to mentor Perry and watch him grow. Perry knows the power of living an unleashed life, and now you can too. I am delighted to recommend his book to you. It will challenge you to be all you can be!"

JOHN C. MAXWELL
Author and speaker

"My friend Perry Noble has experienced the Holy Spirit's transforming power in his life and his church, and he wants the same for you. This book will give you hope that the powerful grace of God is really and truly available to you in Jesus Christ."

MARK DRISCOLL
Founding pastor of Mars Hill Church, cofounder of the Acts 29 church-planting network, founder of Resurgence, and *New York Times* #1 bestselling author

"I love this book! It clearly identifies many of the hidden hindrances to the life God intends for you to live. Each chapter is chock-full of practical wisdom you can immediately apply to experience a breakthrough in areas you thought could never change."

RICK WARREN
Pastor of Saddleback Church and *New York Times* bestselling author of *The Purpose Driven Life*

"Perry Noble is a man of unswerving and uncompromising faith in God. He preaches and leads with boldness and conviction like few other leaders I've met. Now he has turned that passion to the page to help us all learn how to leave normal behind and live a life unleashed."

STEVEN FURTICK
Lead pastor of Elevation Church and author of *Sun Stand Still*

"Perry Noble is one of the most gifted communicators I know, and he has a true pastor's heart. In *Unleash!* he uncompromisingly deals with common life struggles while constantly emphasizing that we can build God's Kingdom only through His grace and His power. I am blessed to know Perry, and you will be blessed by the message the Lord has given him."

ROBERT MORRIS
Senior pastor of Gateway Church and bestselling author of *The Blessed Life*, *From Dream to Destiny,* and *The God I Never Knew*

"If you're tired of doing things halfway and are ready to experience God's power in a new way, you are ready for *Unleash!* In his new book, Perry Noble pushes you to unleash your spiritual potential by going full throttle with Christ. Get ready!"

CRAIG GROESCHEL
Senior pastor of LifeChurch.tv and author of *Soul Detox: Clean Living in a Contaminated World*

UNLEASH!

PERRY NOBLE

BREAKING FREE FROM NORMALCY

TYNDALE HOUSE PUBLISHERS, INC., CAROL STREAM, ILLINOIS 

Visit Tyndale online at www.tyndale.com.

Visit the author's website at www.perrynoble.com.

TYNDALE and Tyndale's quill logo are registered trademarks of Tyndale House Publishers, Inc.

Unleash!: Breaking Free from Normalcy

Designed by Dean H. Renninger

Edited by Stephanie Rische

Published in association with Yates & Yates (www.yates2.com).

Library of Congress Cataloging-in-Publication Data

Noble, Perry.
Unleash! : breaking free from normalcy / Perry Noble.
p. cm.
ISBN 978-1-4143-6679-1 (pbk.)
1. Christian life. 2. David, King of Israel. I. Title.
BV4501.3.N63 2012
248.4—dc23 2012019668

Printed in the United States of America

18 17 16 15 14 13 12
7 6 5 4 3 2 1

CONTENTS

This book is dedicated to all the amazing staff members and "owners" of NewSpring Church. Who knew that what's happening now could ever take place? I'm so honored that Jesus has allowed us to have a front seat and see Ephesians 3:20 take place right in front of our eyes. God is faithful; we have seen great things. But hold on, because the best is yet to come!

FOREWORD

"If God, the Creator of the universe, created us on purpose, with a purpose, and for a purpose, then why in the world would we be willing to settle for anything less?"

That's a really good question.

And that's only one of many good questions you'll be forced to wrestle to the ground in this insightful, entertaining, and practical book by my good friend Perry Noble. The truth is, *Unleash!* should come with a warning label. If it did, it would read something like this: Warning! Every excuse you have for not doing something extraordinary with your life is about to be taken away.

Perry peels away excuses more quickly than a four-year-old peels off a scab. Yeah, I know. That's a bit graphic. But if you know anything about the author of this book, then you know I'm just getting you warmed up for the main event.

Perry and I have been friends for years. In addition to our mutual love for all things Southern, we are joined at the *vision*. Within a year of each other, God birthed in our hearts the desire to create a church for unchurched people. Like Atlanta, Anderson, South Carolina, didn't need just another church. Anderson needed a different kind of church. So in 1999 Perry and his wife, Lucretia, stepped out of their comfort zones and founded NewSpring Church. Under Perry's leadership, NewSpring has become not only one of the fastest-growing churches in the country but also one of the fastest-reproducing churches in the country. If every church leader had a vision for his or her state like Perry does for South Carolina, our nation would be better in every respect.

Knowing Perry the way I do, I'm convinced that the term *unleash* accurately captures the heartbeat and intensity of his life and ministry. Through his disarming transparency and authenticity, Perry has helped to unleash the potential in thousands of people. His unique communication style has captured the imagination of a generation that had given up on church but still longed for purpose. And now, with the publication of his first book, his influence is about to be unleashed to an even broader audience.

Perry writes, "God has a habit of taking average, ordinary people and using them to accomplish extraordinary things." While I doubt anyone who knows Perry would consider him average or ordinary, there is no arguing that what God has done through Perry is extraordinary. More important, when you are finished with this book, you'll be convinced God can do something extraordinary through you, as well.

I have no doubt you'll love this book. But I'm equally convinced that you won't be too far into it before you discover why so many of us love Perry Noble. So get yourself a highlighter. Then put on your big-boy pants. You're about to be unleashed!

Andy Stanley

INTRODUCTION

THERE'S GOT TO BE MORE TO LIFE THAN THIS!

My mother-in-law has a really awesome red Mustang.

A few years ago I borrowed her car for the day when my family and I were visiting my in-laws over the Thanksgiving holidays. I drove the Mustang around for several hours and generally had a blast in it. I ran a few errands, stopped to see some friends, and grabbed a cup of java at a local coffee shop.

Of course, since I typically drive an SUV and am used to riding up a little higher, it took some time to adjust to being so low to the ground. I had to move the seats because I am way taller than my mother-in-law. I played with the radio and found a few stations I liked. I tinkered with the mirrors so I could see behind me. By the end of the day I had come to the conclusion that the car was pretty nice. It got me to where I needed to go, and I had zero complaints. In fact, I'd really enjoyed cruising around in it.

Then, on my way back to my in-laws' house, I had a thought: *This is a Mustang. I wonder if it has any power under the hood.*

Let me pause here and say I have no idea why it took so long for this thought to develop. After all, it was a *Mustang*. I guess I'd been driving a sluggish vehicle for so long that the idea of "blazing a trail" didn't even cross my mind.

With a question like that sitting out there, I obviously had no choice but to stomp on the gas and find out.

Before I knew it, the car was sliding sideways and the tires were screaming for mercy—the Mustang had been unleashed! Had I not let off the gas, I would have lost control completely.

I drove the rest of the way back in stunned silence (which, if you know me, is pretty amazing). I had no idea the car had so much power—the kind of power that could make me nearly mess my pants! I'd been riding around in the vehicle all day, adjusting little things here and there, yet I never took the time to discover whether the car had the ability to leave a few marks on the road.

As I pulled into the driveway of my in-laws' house, I thought, *If I had known this car had that kind of power, I would have driven it a lot differently today—and I would have had a lot more fun while I was at it.*

Unfortunately, a lot of us look at our lives the way I treated that Mustang. As human beings created in the image of God, we are overflowing with unlimited potential, fueled by His limitless power, yet we choose to cruise through life tinkering with the radio and the mirrors, never discovering who God has called us to be. In other words, we never live a life that is truly unleashed.

Two thousand years ago Jesus was raised from the dead, proving what He said in John 16:33—that this world has no power over Him. The world gave its best shot at holding Him down, but three days later He was unleashed from the power of the grave. One of the most fascinating and hard-to-believe things about Christianity is that Jesus lives in us. If the resurrected Son of God lives inside us, that means we, too, can be unleashed from everything that threatens to hold us back from who God wants us to be.

Jesus has made it possible for us to live an unleashed life. Whether we realize it or not, Jesus made the first move. Now He is waiting on us to make the next one.

Jesus made the first move. Now He is waiting on us to make the next one.

Just as I'd been oblivious to the Mustang's power for most of the day, most of us don't even consider living a life that is unleashed. Instead, we settle for average, routine, predictable. But the Bible describes the life of a Christ follower as anything but boring. God doesn't want us to live mediocre, mundane lives.

If that's the case, then why do so many of us wake up in the morning fully expecting nothing more than "normal"?

I'm here to tell you that it's completely possible to live a life beyond normal.

It's completely possible to live with purpose rather than stumble through our days trying to figure out, *Why in the world am I here?*

It's completely possible to live a life marked by freedom and passion rather than one filled with regret and shame.

It's completely possible to live in right relationships with other people rather than let unforgiveness hold us hostage.

It's completely possible for the tragedies in our lives to make us stronger rather than cripple us.

It's completely possible to end strong at the finish line rather than limp along in defeat.

It's completely possible to move beyond normalcy and embrace the abundant life God has for us.

So what are you waiting for? It's time to live a life that is . . . *unleashed*!

CHAPTER 1

SHOWING UP AT THE DANCE

When I was in middle school, I attended every single dance our school had.

Michael Jackson's *Thriller* album was at the top of the charts, and a new form of dancing called break dancing had come into vogue. Almost everyone under the age of eighteen thought they should at least give it a shot (which for many people was a really bad idea).

On the night of a dance I would get my parents to drive me to the school early, and I was usually among the last ones to leave. I tell you seriously, I didn't miss a single one.

Yet in spite of all of the dances I attended, I never actually danced. Ever.

I talked about dancing. I thought about dancing. I watched other people dancing. Quite a few times I almost had the courage to walk onto the dance floor and *try* dancing.

But I didn't. I was one of those guys who was always at the dance but never actually danced.

When I take an honest look at my own life and the lives of the people around me, I have to wonder: are we doing the same thing when it comes to following Christ? Maybe we think about doing something radical for God. Maybe we even dream that one day we'll be more than we are today. But we end up merely standing against the wall, never experiencing the rhythm of God's grace. We don't embrace His promise of a life that is beyond our imagination.

When I read the Gospels, I am consistently amazed by the words of Jesus. When it comes to the kind of life He wants us to live, He made some pretty amazing promises:

> All who came before me were thieves and robbers. But the true sheep did not listen to them. Yes, I am the gate. Those who come in through me will be saved. They will come and go freely and will find good pastures. The thief's purpose is to steal and kill and destroy. My purpose is to give them a rich and satisfying life.
>
> JOHN 10:8-10

> Anyone who believes in me will do the same works I have done, and even greater works, because I am going to be with the Father.
>
> JOHN 14:12

> If you have faith and don't doubt, you can do things like this and much more. You can even say to this mountain, "May you be lifted up and thrown into the sea," and it will happen. You can pray for anything, and if you have faith, you will receive it.
>
> MATTHEW 21:21-22

I could go on, but I'm sure you get the point. God has promised us an abundant life, not a dull one. He said we would do greater things than He did, which is pretty remarkable when we consider that He walked on water, healed a blind guy using mud pies, and fed more than five thousand people with just a little boy's "Happy Meal."

Keep in mind that Jesus also said if we have faith, we can move mountains instead of spending our days feeling crushed by them (see 1 Corinthians 13:2).

Take a second to participate with me in an experiment.

If we have faith, we can move mountains instead of spending our days feeling crushed by them.

Choose a number in your head—any number you want. Go!

What number did you pick? Nearly every time I do this experiment with people, they tell me a number in the ballpark of one to one hundred.

But why?

Why would we pick a number between one and one hundred when we have the option of choosing any number in the world? Why would we not pick 1,284,383?

For many of us, it's a simple and sad answer: we've been programmed to focus on the small and the manageable. We do the same thing with spiritual matters. We focus on what's normal when God has promised He is "able to do immeasurably more than all we ask or imagine" (Ephesians 3:20, NIV).

We all want our lives to count, to matter—and the good news is that God wants that for each one of us as well. The beginning of unleashing the life God wants for us is understanding that there is so much more in store for us than what we are currently experiencing.

Most of us haven't grasped the reality that the resurrected Son of God is dwelling inside us, and therefore we think too small when it comes to the potential God has placed within us. But if we refuse to believe God has something greater in store for us, our chances of becoming unleashed and moving beyond normal are slim to none.

If our view of God is small and manageable—and *normal*—then we will have a small view of what He wants to do in and through us. But if the opposite is true—if we really grasp that God's plan for us is so much bigger and so much more powerful than anything we can imagine—then we will begin to realize the truth in what the apostle Paul promises in Philippians 4:13: "I can do everything through Christ, who gives me strength."

God has called each one of us to embrace life, not merely to endure it. He wants us to have overwhelming victory (see Romans 8:37), to conquer sin and death (see 1 Corinthians 15:57), to not get tired of doing the right thing (see Galatians 6:9), and to make a difference rather than make excuses (see Acts 22:16).

But before we can start living this way, we have to understand two very important truths.

TRUTH #1:
Unleashing your life begins where you are right now.

No matter where you are in life—no matter what you're doing now, what you've done in the past, or what has happened to you—you can begin immediately to take steps toward unleashing the life God has for you. You can start becoming the person God wants you to be rather than feel as if life always gets the best of you.

As we read about Jesus in the Gospels, one thing is clear: He always meets people where they are and then brings them to where they need to be. He never dives into someone's life and immediately starts making religious demands.

When He called Peter, James, and John to follow Him, He didn't give them a list of things they needed to start doing and things they needed to stop doing. He simply invited them to lay down their nets and follow Him. When He called Matthew, a tax collector, to follow Him, He didn't lecture him on the evils of taxation and then tell him he needed a career change. He simply said, "Follow Me," and Matthew responded to the call.

Yes, our actions and habits change after we start following Christ, but that's not the starting point. It's as Jesus walks with us that He shows us who He is and what He wants.

In this book we'll be examining the life of a biblical hero named David. When we read the story of David, it's easy to focus on all the things he accomplished: his epic battle with Goliath, his incredible rise to the throne, his strategic plan for enlarging the borders of Israel. But in doing so, we often miss one of the most important pieces of his journey: the way he arrived on the scene in the first place.

Let's take a look at the first time David appears in the Bible:

> The Lord said to Samuel, "You have mourned long enough for Saul. I have rejected him as king of Israel, so fill your flask with olive oil and go to Bethlehem. Find a man named Jesse who lives there, for I have selected one of his sons to be my king."
>
> But Samuel asked, "How can I do that? If Saul hears about it, he will kill me."
>
> "Take a heifer with you," the Lord replied, "and say that you have come to make a sacrifice to the Lord. Invite Jesse to the sacrifice, and I will show you which of his sons to anoint for me."
>
> So Samuel did as the Lord instructed. When he arrived at Bethlehem, the elders of the town came trembling to meet him. "What's wrong?" they asked. "Do you come in peace?"

"Yes," Samuel replied. "I have come to sacrifice to the LORD. Purify yourselves and come with me to the sacrifice." Then Samuel performed the purification rite for Jesse and his sons and invited them to the sacrifice, too.

When they arrived, Samuel took one look at Eliab and thought, "Surely this is the LORD's anointed!"

But the LORD said to Samuel, "Don't judge by his appearance or height, for I have rejected him. The LORD doesn't see things the way you see them. People judge by outward appearance, but the LORD looks at the heart."

Then Jesse told his son Abinadab to step forward and walk in front of Samuel. But Samuel said, "This is not the one the LORD has chosen." Next Jesse summoned Shimea, but Samuel said, "Neither is this the one the LORD has chosen." In the same way all seven of Jesse's sons were presented to Samuel. But Samuel said to Jesse, "The LORD has not chosen any of these." Then Samuel asked, "Are these all the sons you have?"

"There is still the youngest," Jesse replied. "But he's out in the fields watching the sheep and goats."

"Send for him at once," Samuel said. "We will not sit down to eat until he arrives."

So Jesse sent for him. He was dark and handsome, with beautiful eyes.

And the LORD said, "This is the one; anoint him."

So as David stood there among his brothers, Samuel took the flask of olive oil he had brought and anointed David with the oil. And the Spirit of the LORD came powerfully upon David from that day on. Then Samuel returned to Ramah.

1 SAMUEL 16:1-13

The point I find especially intriguing about this story is that David wasn't out looking to do something great. He woke up one morning, and everything was normal. But in the span of one day, the entire course of his life changed.

It's interesting to note that David wasn't doing the pursuing here; it's the Lord who was seeking out David. God knew that David's life was filled with tremendous potential—David just needed to be unleashed from taking care of sheep so he could transition to leading a nation of people.

After the encounter with God's prophet Samuel, David quickly realized that God had more in store for him than his ordinary circumstances seemed to imply. I imagine from that point on he began watching for the opportunities placed in front of him, although there was no way he could have dreamed all that God had in store.

The Lord was seeking to unleash David so he could do greater things than he ever could have imagined. The same is true for us.

I know what you are thinking: *Okay, Perry, if an old man who claims to be a prophet comes to my house, tells me he's from God, and pours oil over my head, then I'll accept that my life is supposed to be something different from what it is.* (Just my opinion—if that does happen, you might want to call the police.)

That sounds far-fetched, I know, but I believe the Lord has made His plans for us even more obvious than He did for David.

Let's take a look at one of the most powerful yet often unexplored verses in the Bible:

> The Word became human and made his home among us. He was full of unfailing love and faithfulness. And we have seen his glory, the glory of the Father's one and only Son.
>
> JOHN 1:14

God has made Himself evident to us in the person and work of Jesus Christ. If you are a Christian (meaning you understand that sin separates you from God and only Jesus could make the payment to reconcile that relationship), then these things are true about you: (1) God has revealed Himself to you in the living, breathing form of Jesus; (2) He now lives in you; and (3) He really does desire greater things for your life.

Having an unleashed life is completely possible—right now, today. You don't have to get in position for it; God is ready to meet you right where you are.

Are you ready?

TRUTH #2:
Unleashing your life begins by understanding that God wants great things for His children.

I absolutely adore my daughter, Charisse. I used to be a really tough guy who enjoyed movies about car chases and things getting blown up. Now I'm pretty much content to sit on the couch with Charisse, watching the drama of Disney princesses and the adventures of Strawberry Shortcake unfold on our screen.

The Bible is clear that I'm far from being the perfect father (see Matthew 7:9-11), and that is so true. For instance, I have to admit there are times I've lied to my daughter. If you're a parent, you know exactly what I'm talking about. Charisse says she wants to play, but I've been playing all afternoon. And I am so tired. So I say, "I can't right now, baby. I have to go to the bathroom."

Truth be told, I don't have to go to the bathroom at all. It's just the only place where I can sit down to have a little peace and quiet. That is, until I see Charisse's tiny fingers waving at me under the door. "Daddy, are you done yet? Can we play?"

And so, because I love her, I gather up a little more energy and head back to the living room for another tea party or a game of hide-and-seek. I may not be a perfect parent, but I definitely want good things for my daughter. I want her to know how much her daddy loves her.

I once told a friend there is nothing in the world I wouldn't do to hear my little girl laugh. I'm not talking about a giggle or a polite chuckle. I'm talking about the true belly laugh of a child—the kind that can come only as a result of pure joy flowing out of her.

My friend then posed to me one of the most life-changing questions I've ever been asked. "Perry," he said, "if that's how you feel about your daughter and you are what the Bible calls an imperfect father, then why would you ever think your heavenly Father would want anything less for you than for joy to overflow from your heart?"

He was right. God wants to hear us laugh. God is not after our begrudging submission. He is after our joy.

Earlier in this chapter we saw how David arrived on the scene and how God's calling transformed his life from normal to extraordinary. Now let's fast-forward to the end of David's life and note how he never lost sight of the great things God had done for him. Here are some of his last words:

God wants to hear us laugh. God is not after our begrudging submission. He is after our joy.

> David praised the Lord in the presence of the whole assembly:
>
> "O Lord, the God of our ancestor Israel, may you be praised forever and ever! Yours, O Lord, is the greatness, the power, the glory, the victory, and the majesty. Everything in the heavens and on earth is yours, O Lord, and this is your kingdom. We adore you as the one who is

> over all things. Wealth and honor come from you alone, for you rule over everything. Power and might are in your hand, and at your discretion people are made great and given strength.
>
> "O our God, we thank you and praise your glorious name!"
>
> 1 CHRONICLES 29:10-13

In this passage David was preparing the people of Israel to give toward the building of the Temple. What's striking to me is that David didn't sound like he was doing a big fund-raising campaign here. Instead, the text is full of David's amazement at how great and awesome God is. David never forgot who he was or where God had brought him from, and he never lost sight of who God is.

The unleashing of our lives begins when we refuse to believe it's too late for us, when we reject the idea that we're too damaged for God to do anything with, when we stop being obsessed with ourselves. Instead, we must become obsessed with how great God is and how great His plans are for our lives.

The power of unleashing doesn't come when we ask, "What can I do?" The answer to that question always amounts to something that will eventually pass away. The better question is "Who is the Lord, and what does He want to do through me?"

Who are you, Lord?

The apostle Paul (formerly Saul) was another guy who got a pretty direct call to live an unleashed life. He was on his way to persecute Christians when Jesus Himself met him and knocked him flat on the ground. We see this life-changing encounter in Acts 9:3-6:

> As [Saul] was approaching Damascus on this mission, a light from heaven suddenly shone down around him. He

> fell to the ground and heard a voice saying to him, "Saul! Saul! Why are you persecuting me?"
>
> "Who are you, lord?" Saul asked.
>
> And the voice replied, "I am Jesus, the one you are persecuting! Now get up and go into the city, and you will be told what you must do."

Paul went on to accomplish amazing things for God—including writing most of the books of the New Testament—and it all began when Jesus met him exactly where he was. Paul responded by asking the question all of us should ask: "Who are you, Lord?" That is essential, because we will never do what He wants us to do until we understand who He is.

Unleashing our lives is not about convincing God how great our plans are but rather about understanding that we can live the life God has planned for us—right now. It begins when we grasp that God is greater than we give Him credit for. He is after our joy, and ultimately He wants even greater things for us than we do.

We will never do what Jesus wants us to do until we understand who He is.

God had great plans for David that day when He pulled him out of the sheep pen, and He had great plans for Saul when He knocked him flat on his back. He has great plans for us, as well. Once we see who He is, we will find it far easier to surrender to what He says.

Once we've shown up at the dance, we have a choice to make: are we going to stand against the wall, watching other people bust moves, or are we going to get out there on the dance floor ourselves?

God hasn't called His people to stand along the wall as spectators. He wants us to participate with Him in what He is already doing in the world. The reality is that He has already made the first move. He has introduced Himself and offered His hand to us, and now He's just waiting for us to discover who He is. As we see Him more clearly, we will trust Him more fully. We'll follow Him more intentionally. We'll live more completely and abundantly than ever before.

But before we can get there, we need to tackle a few of the common obstacles that hold us back from the full life in store for us.

CHAPTER 2

THE PERFORMANCE TRAP

In 2006 I had two noteworthy achievements: my first marathon . . . and my last.

I've never figured out what inspired me to attempt to run 26.2 miles for no apparent reason. (Since then I've discovered that the first person who ran a marathon died as soon as he completed it!)

I suppose I was looking for a physical challenge at the time, and then there was the incentive of "moral support." When I discussed the idea with a group of friends, they said they'd train with me and fly out to San Diego in June to participate in the event.

I began my training in January, and I can honestly say that over the course of the next six months, I was in the best shape of my life. I was usually the first or second person in my training group to cross the finish line during practice. In fact, I would often complete the run and then go back and find people who were struggling, so I could run in with them.

I trained as effectively as a person could and was as ready for the race as humanly possible. As the date of the marathon grew closer, I felt confident not only that I would finish but also that I would do so in less than four hours. I had prepared so thoroughly that I was sure my performance would be stellar.

Finally it was race day. It was, hands down, one of the most exciting things I'd ever been a part of. There were masses of cheering people on the side of the road, and since it was the Rock 'n' Roll Marathon, there were bands every mile or so playing live music. They had plenty of water and sport drinks available on the side of the road, and I was feeling good. Nothing was going to stop me.

At about mile 13 my legs began to hurt—really hurt. This was a bit unusual because this hadn't happened during my training. I dismissed the pain and continued to push through it. After all, I'd worked hard and put in my time—I was guaranteed a good finish, right?

By mile 19 I had no choice but to start walking. This really bothered me because I'd never walked in any of my training runs. My body began to call me names and curse the day I was born, but I still told myself that my hard work would propel me to an amazing outcome.

At mile 22 I began to consider quitting. I was hurting all over. But I told myself that I had only four miles to go and that all my training had to pay off.

At mile 22.6 I decided to sit on the side of the road for a minute and catch my breath. I lowered myself to the curb, and suddenly everything started spinning and getting blurry.

A guy came up and asked if I was okay. I shook my head. Then he asked if I was going to pass out. I said yes. He asked me when, and I said, "Now."

Then *bam*, my head hit the ground, and I was out cold in the middle of a highway somewhere in San Diego.

Needless to say, I didn't finish the marathon. I was carried to a medical tent, where they loaded me onto an ambulance and carried me to the hospital. I spent the next two hours of my life receiving fluids and getting a CAT scan on my head to make sure I hadn't damaged my brain during the fall. (I would argue that my brain was damaged *before* I passed out, as evidenced by my attempt to run the race in the first place.)

It was one of the most humbling experiences of my life. I had told everyone I knew that I was going to run the race. My entire church had been hearing about it for months. I had bragged to my training group about what I was going to accomplish. And when I had just four miles to go, everything fell apart.

My failure wasn't due to lack of training or lack of effort. I'd done everything I knew to do, yet when it came to accomplishing my goal, I fell short.

My experience with the marathon is a lot like how some of us approach our walk with Christ. We become obsessed with our own performance and hard work, and in doing so, we wear ourselves out spiritually. Despite all our efforts, we fall short of who God is calling us to be. We forget that God isn't looking for a great performance from us; He's looking for us to embrace our position as His children.

We forget that God isn't looking for a great performance from us; He's looking for us to embrace our position as His children.

What are you celebrating?

If you have a child who is no longer in diapers, you understand what it means to go through the potty-training stage. It's one of the most confusing and frustrating times you face as a parent, and you find yourself doing things you never thought you would do.

After several days of facing this challenge, Lucretia and I were sitting in the living room when all of a sudden Charisse announced to us that she had to go poop. Then she promptly walked to the bathroom.

We looked at each other with an incredible amount of hope in our eyes as we waited. At last we heard the magic words: "I'm done."

We both sprinted toward the bathroom to behold the present our little girl had deposited in the toilet for us.

Please stop for just a second and allow the gravity of that previous sentence to hit you. Two fully grown, competent adults literally leaped off the couch to see a pile of poo!

And that's not all. What did we do when we saw it? We did what all parents do when their kids finally accomplish this monumental task—we celebrated! We cheered, gave her hugs and kisses, and acted as if this were the most amazing thing that had ever happened in the history of the world. If you had been in our home, you would have thought our favorite football team had just scored the winning touchdown with no time left on the clock. We absolutely lost our minds.

All over a pile of poo!

Now I'm not saying you shouldn't celebrate the little things with your kids, but unfortunately it reminds me of the way we all—myself included—can get trapped in religion. If we're not careful, we will find ourselves celebrating the crap when we should be celebrating God's goodness in our lives.

I know, I know—the word *crap* may be offensive to you. But stay with me as I explain how real and relevant it is.

The apostle Paul was one of the most religious people on the planet. In fact, when we look at his religious résumé in the book of Philippians, we must admit that it's quite impressive.

> If others have reason for confidence in their own efforts,
> I have even more!

> I was circumcised when I was eight days old. I am a pure-blooded citizen of Israel and a member of the tribe of Benjamin—a real Hebrew if there ever was one! I was a member of the Pharisees, who demand the strictest obedience to the Jewish law. I was so zealous that I harshly persecuted the church. *And as for righteousness, I obeyed the law without fault.*
>
> PHILIPPIANS 3:4-6, EMPHASIS ADDED

Did you catch the last phrase he used to describe himself? *Without fault.* When it came to religious performance, this guy would have won an Academy Award every year. If love for God could be measured by how well a person performed, then no one could have touched Paul.

But Paul's next words will rock anyone who depends on their performance to try to measure up with God:

> I once thought these things were valuable, but now I consider them worthless because of what Christ has done. Yes, everything else is worthless when compared with the infinite value of knowing Christ Jesus my Lord. For his sake I have discarded everything else, *counting it all as garbage*, so that I could gain Christ and become one with him. I no longer count on my own righteousness through obeying the law; rather, I become righteous through faith in Christ. For God's way of making us right with himself depends on faith.
>
> PHILIPPIANS 3:7-9, EMPHASIS ADDED

I want to draw your attention specifically to the word *garbage* in verse 8. The Greek word used by Paul is *skubala*—the word commonly used in that time to describe human excrement.

I know it's extreme, but if the apostle Paul, under the inspiration of the Holy Spirit, wrote that his religious performance was nothing more than a pile of poo, then we have to acknowledge that this must be something God feels strongly about.

Basically Paul is saying that when he was unleashed to the idea of God's amazing grace, he ceased celebrating the crap in his life and began celebrating God's goodness.

Earning God's love

Scripture is full of examples of people who were chosen by God for a specific purpose. Let's take another look at David's life in 1 Samuel 17:1-3:

> The Philistines now mustered their army for battle and camped between Socoh in Judah and Azekah at Ephes-dammim. Saul countered by gathering his Israelite troops near the valley of Elah. So the Philistines and Israelites faced each other on opposite hills, with the valley between them.

When we read the story of David and Goliath, most of us are tempted to sort of skim over these verses and get to the "good stuff" about flinging rocks and giants getting their rear ends kicked. But before we go any further, I think it's important to reflect on how loaded these verses are.

The Bible is clear that there are two opposing sides in this battle. The text paints a picture of two massive hills, with the Israelites occupying one hill and the Philistines occupying the other.

We could say that on one hill were the children of God and on the other hill were the enemies of God. Which brings us to this critical question: what was the one thing that distinguished the

Israelites from the Philistines? What made them so special compared with their neighbors?

It wasn't their weaponry; it wasn't their armor style. It wasn't that they had performed so well that God somehow felt obligated to place them on a pedestal.

The answer is simple: it was nothing more than the undeserved grace of God!

One of the most fascinating things about the Bible is that it doesn't attempt to cover up the shortcomings of God's people. In fact, every "Bible hero" we tend to lift up as some sort of saint had issues to battle through, just as we do. Based on the Israelites' track record of sin and brokenness, we know there wasn't anything impressive or special about them. They were God's children not because they were good but rather because *He* is good.

The same thing is true for those of us who are Christians today. Because of who Jesus is and what He did for us on the cross, everyone has access to "God's hill"—to being His child. We can live a life that is unleashed because of whose we are, not who we are.

The story of the Israelites doesn't unfold as you might expect for people who have been chosen as God's special people. The nation began when God called Abram out of a pagan land to follow Him (see Genesis 12). This wasn't because of anything Abram had done, I might add. According to the Bible, he was an ordinary man living in a society that happened to be polytheistic. He wasn't necessarily seeking God or trying to get His attention.

We can live a life that is unleashed because of *whose* we are, not *who* we are.

But in His mercy, God unleashed Abraham! Abraham was just doing his own thing in his own country, and out of nowhere God appeared to him and said He was going to make Abraham famous and bless the whole world through him.

Eventually Abram (later renamed Abraham) had Isaac, Isaac had Jacob, and then Jacob had twelve sons—most of whom were not guys a father would want his daughter to bring home! (Just to give you an idea, one of them had sex with his daughter-in-law; ten of them conspired to kill their own brother; and at one point they became so angry and vengeful that they deceived and killed all the men in an entire city.)

Jacob and his descendants ended up moving to Egypt, were eventually enslaved by the Egyptians, and stayed that way for 430 years . . . until God raised up a man named Moses to lead them out of slavery.

We need to stop for a moment and examine why God set the Israelites free from slavery. Was it because they started following some set of religious rules? No. In fact, the Ten Commandments hadn't even been given yet. Was it because of their impeccable moral performance? Nope—they had their share of sins and failures. Could it have been because they cracked some sort of religious formula that forced God to perform miracles for them?

No, not even close. They were slaves! The only thing a slave can do every day is be a slave. Day in and day out, they were held captive by people more powerful than they were. They'd done nothing to earn God's approval, yet God chose to unleash them.

And what happened once the Israelites were set free from slavery? Did they do anything to deserve His continued love and blessings after that?

Absolutely not! As we read about their long journey through the desert into the Promised Land, we see that they grumbled against God, complained to Moses, practiced idolatry, committed acts of sexual immorality, and were downright unfaithful to the God who had set them free. Yet in spite of all this, God's love for them never stopped and never waned. His love was based not on their performance but rather on their position as His children.

If you are in Christ, the same thing that was true for the Israelites and for David is true for you. It was God who set you free in the first place—not based on your own merits but simply because He loved you. And the same is true for you after you become a Christian. He continues to shower you with His love and blessings simply because you are His beloved child.

We can't do a single thing to earn God's love. Earning God's love is a spiritual impossibility—no one in the history of humankind has ever been able to accomplish that task. God's love cannot be achieved; it can only be received.

God's love cannot be achieved; it can only be received.

My encounter with His unleashing grace

It's easy for us to start believing our performance somehow determines whether or not God loves us, even when our faith begins with a true encounter with grace. That's what happened to me.

I received Christ into my life on May 27, 1990. I will never forget that day.

A friend of mine had been inviting me to church for months, and I finally agreed to attend with him because he informed me there were "really hot girls" there. Over the period of the next three months, something "weird" started taking place: I actually began to listen to the messages. I finally understood the gospel—that I was a sinner, separated from God and in desperate need of a Savior. I finally understood that I needed to submit my life to Christ.

At first I tried to dismiss this thought, as I had walked an aisle when I was five years old and I'd always considered that to be when I'd received Christ into my life. However, the more I reflected on that event, the more I realized how little I'd truly grasped at the time.

It was a Sunday night, and the preacher had been ranting for over an hour about why Elvis Presley was going to hell. It was the late '70s, and in my home church back then, Elvis was a common target for who was on the "hell express."

I should tell you that even now I have an incredibly hard time focusing on something for more than five consecutive seconds (just imagine me at the age of five!), so when the invitation was given for people to come to the altar and pray, I saw it as an opportunity to get up and move. I seized it.

As I was "praying" at the altar, the preacher put his hand on my shoulder and asked me if I wanted to go to heaven or hell (which is an awesome question to ask a five-year-old). I was pretty scared of the preacher, as he was a large man. And when I say large, I mean he could have gone bear hunting with a switch! I began to cry because I didn't know if he was offering me the option to go right then or later, and he took advantage of my pause to claim, "The Spirit is on you!" I didn't know exactly what that meant, but I did know I was about to wet myself over the whole idea of going to hell.

He told me to repeat a prayer after him, so I did. After the prayer he stood me in front of the church and told everyone I was going to go to heaven. I remember thinking, Well, you literally just scared the hell out of me, so there really is no other option. I had no idea what had just taken place. I did not understand sin, separation from God, or that Jesus had taken my place on the cross. All I knew was that I'd prayed a prayer and everyone seemed excited about it. The church even gave me a Bible with my name in it. For years I considered that jacked-up experience to be my official conversion.

Fast-forward fourteen years to the fall of 1989, when I started going to church with my friend. I wasn't there because I thought I needed to get saved—I just enjoyed being there and wanted to meet the promised hot girls. The church youth group was going on a mission trip that summer, so I signed up, having no idea that doing so meant I was automatically enrolled in what they referred to as their youth choir.

One Sunday night before the evening service began, we were having choir practice in preparation for the upcoming trip. We were singing the song "Do I Trust You, Lord?" I remember singing the words and trying to harmonize when out of nowhere I felt the Lord saying to me, "You can't trust Me because you do not know Me."

I immediately stopped singing and sat down. I couldn't speak. In an instant, everything I'd been hearing in church made sense. I had sinned, my sin had separated me from God, and no amount of good works could ever make up for the sin in me. It was only through surrendering my life to Christ that I could be made right with God.

After choir practice I found the nearest church staff member and told him I needed to ask Christ into my life. I knelt to do that, and when I stood up, I was a changed man.

To say that God changed me would be an understatement. I knew enough about the Bible to realize that my soul had been power washed and I was a brand-new person. But I wasn't the only one who could sense the difference. People who had known me for any length of time started commenting on the changes that were quickly becoming noticeable in my life.

Before I met Christ, I had a porn addiction. I began viewing porn at the age of twelve, and it had been a regular part of my life for more than six years. I'd never felt any sort of conviction over this—I just saw it as a completely natural part of my life.

However, after receiving Christ, I had this overwhelming thought: I really need to stop looking at porn. No one preached a sermon on it. No one sat me down and told me I was now in the "no porn club." It was just something that I knew was going to have to go in my life.

Another change that took place was with my temper. In the past when I was angry with someone or didn't get my way, I would fly off the handle and either cuss them out or try to punch them. However, after I turned my life over to Jesus, He immediately began convicting me about my anger issues and teaching me to respond with patience and grace. Once again, no one sat me down and told me, "Perry, you can't go around and punch people in the throat when they make you mad." I just knew it was something that needed to change.

The resurrected Son of God had come to live inside me, and the change was starting to become evident. However, it wasn't long before I fell into the performance trap and bound myself in religious chains.

God loves everyone . . . but I'm His favorite.

Somewhere along the way I started to buy into the idea that God's love for me was based not on His grace but rather on my effort to earn His love. Believing that lie held me hostage to what can be one of the most damaging enemies of the unleashed life: religion.

Gradually my perspective got warped, and instead of focusing on what God was doing in my life, I poured my energy into adhering to self-imposed rules, assuming that this would make me more acceptable and loved in His sight. In doing so, I ceased to live for the things that really matter to God and began to hyper-focus on the things that mattered to *me*!

If you had asked me to describe my "new Christian life" about three years after I received Christ, I would have said the following:

- "I don't listen to secular music."
- "I don't drink any sort of alcohol."
- "I don't cuss."
- "I read my Bible every day."

- "I pray every day."
- "I go to church multiple times a week."
- "I have an accountability partner."
- "I memorize Scripture."
- "I am involved in multiple Bible studies."

Notice the word that starts out each item on the list: *I*!

As I think back on this period in my life, I realize that the Lord's words in Isaiah are a perfect description of me.

> These people say they are mine.
> They honor me with their lips,
> but their *hearts* are far from me.
> And their worship of me
> is nothing but man-made rules learned by rote.
>
> ISAIAH 29:13, EMPHASIS ADDED

I did all the "right things." I followed all the rules. I bowed down to the religious idol of performance. I loved Jesus with my head, and all the while I hadn't fully trusted my heart to Him. As a result, I wasn't free to love Him with everything I had.

For nearly fifteen years I wrestled with the performance trap. I thought there was no way God could love me simply because I was His child. I was sure His love was conditional on how I behaved. As a result, I read my Bible, shared Christ, and did good things—not out of an overflow of love but rather out of fear and insecurity. I was sure that if I didn't do the right things, God would turn His back on me.

I had let my identity become wrapped up in my performance rather than in my position as His child.

There are two main problems with this. The first is that if

something on our list ever gets out of whack, we feel as if God doesn't love us.

Here's what that looked like in my life. If for some reason I didn't read my Bible one morning, by lunchtime I was absolutely convinced that I was no longer in the realm of God's love. If I didn't spend at least thirty minutes in prayer, I was plagued by guilt. I reasoned, *If I can spend thirty minutes watching television, why can't I spend that much time praying?*

I was so messed up about this that I blamed anything bad that happened on my poor performance and figured God was getting even with me for something I'd done wrong. One time in particular stands out and shows just how ridiculous my mind-set had become.

I hit a deer really late at night on a country road in the middle of nowhere. The accident caused hundreds of dollars in damage to my car, and it was quite an ordeal to get it repaired. Here's the thing—I truly thought the reason I'd hit the deer was that at the time I was listening to "secular music." I had secretly bought a Travis Tritt tape and had just put it in so I could sing "Here's a Quarter" at the top of my lungs. I was thirty seconds into the song when the leaping beast came dashing out of the woods, apparently executing the wrath of God on my life because of my immoral music selection.

I lived with a defeated mind-set for quite a while after that, falsely believing God had sent the deer to judge me because I was listening to country music rather than Christian music.

I know now that's a messed-up way of seeing God, but that's how skewed my perspective had become. In my effort to dot all the i's and cross all the t's when it came to my religious performance, I locked myself in a prison of my own making. I didn't realize I was holding myself back from the unleashed life Jesus promises.

Before we can embrace the abundant life God has called us to, we have to understand this concept: His love is *not* based on our performance. In fact, the Bible says in Isaiah 64:6 that even our "righteous" acts (how we act on those days when we seem to be getting everything right) are like filthy rags in His sight.

Seriously, where do we get the idea we can impress God with anything we do?

And yet we so easily fall into the lie that if we aren't living up to a certain standard, God doesn't love us.

But hear this: you cannot out-sin the grace of God. Ever! This is probably the truest statement I've ever made from the pulpit. It's probably also the one I've gotten the most flak about. But don't take it from me—listen to what the Bible says:

> I am convinced that nothing can ever separate us from God's love. Neither death nor life, neither angels nor demons, neither our fears for today nor our worries about tomorrow—not even the powers of hell can separate us from God's love. No power in the sky above or in the earth below—indeed, nothing in all creation will ever be able to separate us from the love of God that is revealed in Christ Jesus our Lord.
>
> ROMANS 8:38-39

God's love is in Christ, *not* in our performance.

Let's take a look at Peter, one of Jesus' disciples. He followed Jesus for three years and was one of the friends in Jesus' inner circle. He was the first apostle to confess that Jesus was the Messiah and even promised that he would die with Him. Yet when it all hit the fan, Peter ran away, abandoning Christ and outright denying he knew Him.

If God's love were based on performance, Peter blew it for sure. He was out, off the team, permanently outside the Lord's care.

But we see in Scripture that Jesus not only forgave Peter but also allowed him to preach the gospel at a huge gathering after Jesus' resurrection (see Acts 2). Jesus didn't fire Peter after his denial—He put him in charge of the church (see Matthew 16:18). And it certainly wasn't because of Peter's performance; it was only because of the unleashing grace of God.

That same unleashing grace is available for each of us, too.

God brought this truth home to me during a recent conversation with my four-year-old daughter, Charisse.

We were driving down the road, and I asked her, "Charisse, did you know your daddy loves you?"

"Yes, sir," she replied.

"How much do you think your daddy loves you?"

In the rearview mirror I could see her holding out her arms as wide open as they would go. "This much," she said.

Then I asked her, "Do you know *why* your daddy loves you?"

She had a confused look on her face and told me no, she didn't.

"Charisse," I said, "I love you because you are my daughter. That's it."

She smiled, so I asked another question: "Can Daddy ever stop loving you?"

"No, sir." She smiled again.

"And why not?"

"Because," she said, "I will always be your daughter."

She gets it. Do you?

If you are in Christ, you are loved because you are His. Not because of anything you've done.

The second problem with basing our identity on our performance is that it causes us to look down on people we perceive aren't as "morally superior" as we are. (Which has done Christianity *so* much good!)

When I measured my performance compared against other

people's, I looked down on them and saw myself as "holier" than they were. I concluded not only that I loved God more than they did but also that God probably loved me more than He loved them.

If you are in Christ, you are loved because you are His. Not because of anything you've done.

I am ashamed to admit that this was my attitude: *God loves everyone . . . but I'm His favorite.*

The Bible calls this kind of attitude *pride*, and it also says that God hates pride. As a friend of mine once said, "Pride is the sin that got Satan kicked out of heaven and will actually earn us all a cut in the line to hell."

When we get caught up in the performance mind-set, we celebrate the wrong thing—we focus on our own goodness instead of on God's. Doing so is nothing less than thumbing our noses at God's unleashing grace and celebrating a bunch of, er, *skubala*.

Moving past the religious latrine

People who are in Christ are not perfect—they are just forgiven because of God's unleashing grace. The one thing that separates Christians from non-Christians is the cross of Christ—that's it.

Being in ministry for more than twenty years now has opened my eyes to the reality that people's lives on either side of the cross are messy. The difference is that those of us who are in Christ can move past the mess if we understand that our mess doesn't disqualify us for His love. If we ever lose sight of that, we will find ourselves constantly gathering around the religious latrine, celebrating our own performance and neglecting to celebrate the goodness of God.

I know the fear here. Some people argue that if we really believe in God's unleashing grace, that He loves us—period—not because of our behavior but because of His character, people will go out and do whatever they want.

I understand that fear. It was mine as well at one time. But the truth is, when we really understand the amazing grace of God and that He loves us no matter what, it will motivate us to do not whatever we want but whatever He wants.

When I finally began to understand and embrace grace in its true form, it didn't give me a free pass to live carelessly and use grace as an excuse to sin. Rather, it motivated me to surrender every aspect of my life to God, because I'd never been loved and accepted that way—by anyone!

When we really understand the amazing grace of God and that He loves us no matter what, it will motivate us to do not whatever we want but whatever He wants.

Embracing this God-focused mind-set completely revolutionized my life. As a result, I began to read the Bible not because I felt I had to in order to win God's approval but rather because I wanted to know more about the God who loved me unconditionally. I began to pray not because I felt guilty if I didn't but because I wanted to connect with the God who had gone out of His way to connect with me.

These practices were no longer duties for me; they were delights. I was finally starting to understand that if I am in Christ, God cannot love me any more, and He will not love me any less. No matter what. And it's only when we embrace that truth that the true unleashing can begin.

CHAPTER 3

MOVING PAST YOUR PAST

I will never forget the worst day of my life.

I was in the sixth grade, and let's just say I was not the smallest kid in my class. Truth be told, I was quite large.

Our class was doing an assessment in PE to see how physically fit we were. The tests included push-ups, sit-ups, pull-ups, and so on. However, right before the physical fitness tests, we went to lunch, where on that particular day we happened to have burritos.

As soon as we arrived at PE class, the teacher announced that the first thing we would be testing was how many sit-ups we could do in one minute. She asked us to partner up by numbering off (1, 2, 1, 2), and the person I just happened to end up with was, in my opinion, the prettiest girl in the entire class: Tara Ann.

If you asked me, she wasn't just the prettiest girl in the class; she was the prettiest girl on the entire planet. Tara Ann was also funny and smart, and on that day she happened to be wearing a cheerleading outfit.

When it became obvious that she was going to be my sit-up partner, I was so pumped. I just knew I was going to put forth so much effort and work so hard that she would be in awe of my superior sit-up skills and want to be my girl forever.

So I got on the ground, and Tara Ann held my feet. I was so excited I started shaking. This was it—my one shot at impressing the girl who had captivated my attention all year long. (Did I mention we had just eaten lunch? And that I'd had a burrito? Anyone see a train wreck coming?)

The PE teacher blew the whistle, and I gave it every ounce of effort I had. One, two . . . and then, on the third sit-up, with no warning whatsoever, I . . . uh . . .

Let's just say I parted her hair. (For those who still might not understand, let me be blunt: I passed gas, and it was loud!)

I will never forget the look Tara Ann gave me. I knew from that moment on it would never work between us. I was absolutely mortified that I had farted in the face of the most attractive girl I had ever seen.

I never forgot that moment.

When we got to middle school, we certainly didn't run in the same circles, but I would see her every so often. Every time I did, I would think back to the awful experience I'd put her through in PE class "back in the day."

When we got to high school, the same thing happened. I distinctly remember her walking by me in the hallway one day. As she did, I said to myself, Dude, you are such a loser—you ripped one off in her face.

And then there was my ten-year high school reunion. (I promise I'm not making this up!) I went to my old high school on Friday night for the football game, and my graduating class was supposed to meet behind the press box at halftime. Sure enough, the first person who walked up to me, a big smile on her face, was Tara Ann. *The* Tara Ann. She said, "Hey, Perry, do you remember me?"

How in the world could I ever forget? I thought. *I'm the guy who ruined your sixth grade year!*

The funny thing is, even though I'd allowed that one bad event to define every interaction I had with Tara Ann, she didn't seem to remember it at all.

I'm quite sure no one in the class that day thought about that little incident any longer than five minutes. Heck, I'd even be willing to bet Tara Ann finally got past it after some time and a few counseling sessions.

For me, however, it was the one thing that dominated my mind every time I saw her. I couldn't enjoy any type of normal interaction, let alone relationship, with her because of what had happened in the past.

Unfortunately, the same thing is true for so many of us when it comes to our spiritual lives. We can't move on to the future God has for us if we are dominated by the mistakes of our past.

If you don't get anything else from this chapter, then please get this: if you don't let your past die, then it won't let you live. Period.

If you don't let your past die, then it won't let you live.

Once you surrender your life to Christ, your identity is not in what you have done but rather by what Jesus has done for you on the cross. In other words, you can't find your identity in who you used to be but rather in who you are now in Christ. Scripture says in 2 Corinthians 5:17 that we are brand-new people—the old is gone and the new has come.

When we last left the story of David in 1 Samuel, we saw that an epic battle was about to take place, with the forces of darkness on one side and the children of God on the other. It was a time of tremendous uncertainty and fear for the Israelites, and out of that setting we see the following scene.

> Goliath, a Philistine champion from Gath, came out of the Philistine ranks to face the forces of Israel. He was over nine feet tall! He wore a bronze helmet, and his bronze coat of mail weighed 125 pounds. He also wore bronze leg armor, and he carried a bronze javelin on his shoulder. The shaft of his spear was as heavy and thick as a weaver's beam, tipped with an iron spearhead that weighed 15 pounds. His armor bearer walked ahead of him carrying a shield. Goliath stood and shouted a taunt across to the Israelites. "Why are you all coming out to fight?" he called. "I am the Philistine champion, but you are only the servants of Saul. Choose one man to come down here and fight me!"
>
> 1 SAMUEL 17:4-8

Even if you've heard this story before, let's not gloss over what the text says.

First of all, Goliath was enormous. Most scholars agree that he was about nine feet nine inches tall. Whoa. That's two feet and eight inches taller than Shaquille O'Neal, one of the tallest, most dominant players to ever play in the NBA. Goliath was most likely the largest enemy the Israelites had ever had to deal with.

And just to give you a mental picture of this guy, his coat of armor weighed around 125 pounds, and the tip of his spear alone weighed fifteen pounds. One look at this giant and no one was really motivated to fight. They were ready to run.

For many of us, our past mistakes loom as large as Goliath. No matter what we do, no matter how many times we say we're sorry, no matter how many Bible verses we read or how many worship songs we sing, our past always seems to be there, towering over us like a large enemy we just can't figure out how to bring down.

As if Goliath's enormous size weren't enough, he apparently spent his spare time shouting insults at the Israelites, threatening that he would completely destroy them. This was, hands down, the most intimidating situation the Israelite army had ever faced.

> Goliath stood and shouted a taunt across to the Israelites. "Why are you all coming out to fight?" he called. "I am the Philistine champion, but you are only the servants of Saul. Choose one man to come down here and fight me! If he kills me, then we will be your slaves. But if I kill him, you will be our slaves! I defy the armies of Israel today! Send me a man who will fight me!" When Saul and the Israelites heard this, they were terrified and deeply shaken.
>
> 1 SAMUEL 17:8-11

This had to be frustrating for the Israelites, to say the least. God had set them free from slavery in Egypt hundreds of years before, and yet in this story we see them under the thumb of another enemy, the Philistines. This enemy was manipulative and intimidating, and on top of that, *loud*. The Israelites must have become so obsessed with Goliath's taunts and insults that they could no longer hear the voice of God.

This happens to us as well, doesn't it? Not only is our past large and intimidating, but it also yells at us, constantly reminding us of our shortcomings and telling us we can never live an unleashed life because of all the mistakes we've made. I've learned from personal experience that one of the quickest ways to forget what God says about me is to focus on what the enemy says about me.

Any number of triggers can bring the giant of our past out to taunt us. Sometimes it happens when we see a friend from a "former life." Other times, movies or songs jog our memories about something we've done wrong. In other cases regrets and painful memories pop into our minds out of nowhere, and along with them come feelings of guilt, condemnation, and shame.

> For forty days, every morning and evening, the Philistine champion strutted in front of the Israelite army.
> 1 SAMUEL 17:16

Did you catch that? Goliath came out every morning and every evening for forty days—that means that on at least eighty occasions the Israelites were dominated by this voice of intimidation and manipulation. I'm quite sure by this point they were so obsessed with the giant that they had begun to believe freedom wasn't even possible.

Some of us have come to the same conclusion. We've allowed ourselves to become so obsessed with the giant of our past that we can't live in the freedom and joy Jesus intends for us. We've allowed fear to define us rather than God.

If we want to be unleashed—if we want to live the abundant life Jesus promised—then we can't allow what used to defeat us to define us.

If we want to be unleashed—if we want to live the abundant life Jesus promised—then we can't allow what used to defeat us to define us. That's simply not who we are anymore. That may be who we were, but it's not who we are in Christ.

If we are ever going to move beyond our past, we need to accept these three unleashing truths found in God's Word.

TRUTH #1: In Christ you are completely forgiven.

I have battled with weight issues all my life. There was a time when I wore a size 50 in the waist and weighed more than three hundred pounds. To put it mildly, I was unhealthy and out of shape.

Today the opposite is true—I'm in great shape and at a healthy weight. However, since I spent so much of my past being overweight, I often battle with feeling obese.

It's insane really—no one today would think of me as obese, and I can see in the mirror that I'm exercising and taking care of myself.

But there are days when I just don't feel in shape because of my past. What I've had to come to terms with is the realization that my feelings don't always tell the truth. We can't build the foundation of our lives on something as fickle as emotion.

When it comes down to it, most of us have trouble getting beyond our past because we don't really believe God forgives us. Yes, we hear about forgiveness and maybe even give lip service to it, but deep down few of us accept it.

I think the reason most of us can't grasp the unleashing forgiveness of God is because we have a hard time forgiving others ourselves. Let me explain.

In 2005 I bought a brand-new GMC Yukon. I had never owned a brand-new car before, so this was quite a special purchase for me.

One evening I went to a local fast-food restaurant for a meeting, and when I came out, it was immediately obvious that another car had smashed into mine in the parking lot.

I tried to not panic. Well, I thought, maybe they hit my car and didn't want to cause a huge scene in the restaurant, so they put a note on my windshield with their name and number on it so we can get this all straightened out.

I got to my car and—you guessed it—no note.

To say I was angry would be an understatement. I couldn't believe someone would dent my car and just walk away. Maybe some people would say at this point, "You should have stopped and prayed for them." I did all right—I took one of David's prayers right out of the book of Psalms: "O LORD . . . shatter the teeth of the wicked!" (Psalm 3:7).

Every time I walked by my car and saw the dent, I became angry. I couldn't get over the fact that someone would do that kind of damage and not take responsibility for it.

As we look back over the "dents" in our lives and our struggle to forgive those who have damaged us, we tend to conclude that God must struggle to forgive us as well. But Scripture makes it clear that our lives are identified not by the dents but rather by the death Christ died on the cross. Through trusting Him and receiving His forgiveness, we are made brand new, and there are no longer any dents on us.

The apostle Paul says it this way: "He is so rich in kindness and grace that he purchased our freedom with the blood of his Son and forgave our sins" (Ephesians 1:7). According to this verse (and the rest of the Bible, for that matter), forgiveness is not achieved but rather *received*. We can't work for forgiveness. We can't take our damaged lives to the "body shop," trying to beat the dents out on our own and make it look like nothing ever happened.

There is only one way to deal with our brokenness, and that's to accept the forgiveness Jesus offers.

This can be a tough truth to swallow because many times we don't feel forgiven. But true forgiveness isn't a feeling; it's a reality (see 1 John 3:20). God created each of us knowing full well how we'd rebel against Him. Even before we were born, He made arrangements to pick up the bill for our sin since He knew we'd be unable to do so on our own. Just because we may not feel forgiven at times doesn't change the fact that in Christ, God has forgiven all our sin. Because our past has been paid for, our potential is unlimited.

I have to be honest, though—I still struggle with not feeling forgiven.

One day recently I was in my car listening to the '80s station on XM radio when a famous song by the band Milli Vanilli came on. I enjoyed it for a few seconds, and then all of a sudden it brought back a time when I was in high school at a place I should not have been, doing some things I should not have been doing.

The memories were painful—so much so that I actually winced. The voice of my past was loud and accusatory, and for several minutes I felt the weight of guilt and condemnation on me.

How in the world is a person supposed to fight through this? I thought. I felt helpless—trapped by something I'd done decades earlier. After all, the past is what it is, and it cannot be altered, no matter how much we attempt to wish it away.

Then I thought about the reality of Ephesians 1:7—that through Christ's sacrifice on the cross, all my sins have been completely paid for. I felt the battle raging in my mind as I wrestled to believe the reality of Scripture over what I was feeling. I didn't find relief until I began saying out loud, "That sin was paid for by Jesus on the cross. In Him I am completely forgiven."

Maybe you don't wrestle with a shady past. Maybe you don't have any skeletons in your closet. Maybe you aren't haunted by past decisions you've made. And yet you still don't feel like you're living a life that is unleashed.

I would like to suggest that even if your life looks pretty good on the outside, all of us are born sinful (see Romans 3:23). That means all of us are in need of God's forgiveness.

One of the things that can be hard for people from a churched background to grasp is that we are all separated from God. We often hear radical testimonies that go something like this: "I began smoking crayons and sniffing Elmer's glue when I was three years old, I committed my first murder in the first grade, and I sold drugs for a living in the fourth grade. Then one day I met Jesus, and He made it all better!"

Okay, maybe that's a little over the top, but it does seem like the more dramatic the testimony, the more in awe we are. The difficulty comes when we hear these stories and start assuming we're something special. Wow, we think, I've never sold drugs or killed anyone or committed adultery. I guess I'm good!

Nothing could be further from the truth.

We are all rule breakers! Even on our best day we couldn't keep all the Ten Commandments.

"Wait!" you may argue. "I can!"

Really? Are you sure?

What about the one where God says not to dishonor your father and your mother? (If you were ever a teenager, you completely blew it there, didn't you?)

What about where God says not to murder? You might want to push back there, confident you'd never kill anyone. But what about when Jesus says in the Sermon on the Mount that having hatred in our hearts toward someone is the same as murder?

And what about the commandment that says we should not covet? I break this one every time I go to a friend's house and see that they have recently purchased a new big-screen, super-duper HD television. I immediately become dissatisfied with mine. Guilty as charged. And I'm guessing I'm not alone in this.

The list goes on: I'd venture to say every one of us has lied, gossiped, and turned a blind eye to someone in need. All of us, from the worst sinner on the planet to someone who was practically born on the church altar, need to understand that in Christ, and Christ alone, we are completely forgiven and made right with God.

Our sinful behavior doesn't surprise God. He will never look at us and say, "I can't believe you did that." Before time began, He knew what we would do, and He knew what our sin would cost Him. But He chose to save us anyway. There is unleashing power in that kind of forgiveness.

TRUTH #2: In Christ you are valuable.

I was robbed once.

Just after high school graduation I worked as a cashier for a restaurant. One Saturday afternoon a man came in wearing a gray sweatshirt with the hood pulled over his head, a black jacket, sunglasses, and black gloves. I remember thinking, *If I were going to rob a place, that's exactly how I would dress!* It was a funny thought . . . until he pulled out the largest knife I'd ever seen and demanded that I open the cash drawer.

In that moment I made two decisions. (1) He could have the money in the register. Seriously, I didn't wrestle with that choice at all. There was not one ounce of desire in me to play the hero. (2) He wasn't getting my wallet, and I would fight him if he tried.

Why was I so passionate about my wallet? Trust me, it wasn't because I had any money in it. Rather, it was because my driver's license was there, and I would rather have been stabbed by that guy than go to the DMV to get a new license.

My driver's license, as you might be able to tell, was very valuable to me.

We all have things we consider valuable and will do just about anything to protect. Maybe for you it's your phone, your glasses, or your child. Perhaps it's when we're in danger of losing any of those things that we realize just how valuable it is.

If something is precious to us, we take care of it. And if it happens to go missing, we pursue it with relentless passion.

That's exactly how God views us. He sees us as His most valuable possessions, and He will do whatever it takes to protect us and pursue us. We can't live a truly unleashed life until we begin to understand how precious we are to God.

The facts of God's Word always trump the feelings in our hearts.

Let me be honest here: there are times when I struggle to believe I'm valuable to God. Especially when I'm haunted by my past and all the stupid mistakes I've made. However, as we mature in following Christ, we begin to believe what God's Word says over the way we feel. The facts of God's Word always trump the feelings in our hearts.

And God's Word says that each one of us is valuable to Him. Check out this Scripture passage with me:

> All praise to God, the Father of our Lord Jesus Christ, who has blessed us with every spiritual blessing in the heavenly realms because we are united with Christ. Even before he made the world, God loved us and chose us in Christ to be holy and without fault in his eyes. . . .
>
> Furthermore, because we are united with Christ, we have received an inheritance from God, for he chose us in advance, and he makes everything work out according to his plan.
>
> EPHESIANS 1:3-4, 11

These verses have sparked a lot of theological controversy over the years; however, I want to focus on a simple truth here: the Bible clearly says that God—the Creator of the universe, the Alpha and the Omega, the Beginning and the End—chose us. And if God chose you, that makes you valuable—no matter what you've done, no matter what has happened in your past.

In Christ, our value is determined not by what we have done but rather by what Christ did for us on the cross.

I can hear your arguments right now: "Perry, you don't know my story. I'm sure some people are valuable to God, but not me. There's no way He could see me as important after the things I've done."

What we have to understand is that the value of something is determined by the price someone is willing to pay for it.

I love football, and I always enjoy following the NFL draft. In 2010 I had a friend who was being drafted, so I watched that draft class with even more interest than usual.

The number one draft pick that year was a young man by the name of Sam Bradford, from Oklahoma University. He was drafted by the St. Louis Rams and was signed to play for six years . . . and $78 million.

Please read that figure again—*$78 million.*

Question: do you think Sam Bradford mattered to the St. Louis Rams? Do you think they cared about his health? His development? His whereabouts?

Absolutely! And why did they happen to care so much? Simple—because they'd paid an incredible price for him.

If you are in Christ, you are valuable to God because He paid an incredible price for you—the life of His own Son.

If you are in Christ, you are valuable to God because He paid an incredible price for you—the life of His own Son. In Christ your worth is determined not by your past performance, not by the brand of jeans you wear, not by the house you live in, or even by your religious résumé. Your value is determined by the fact that God gave His only Son for you.

TRUTH #3: In Christ you are unconditionally loved.

As much as I hate to admit it, my love has conditions . . . and so does yours.

Let's face it: there are some people who are just hard to love. Don't lie—you know it's true.

For me personally, it's hard to love "close talkers"—you know, those people who think they have to get all up in your grill. You can't even hear what they're saying because you want to shove a breath mint into their mouth.

It's also hard for me to love people who come for a visit and refuse to leave. After you eat dinner, you clean up and tell them it was nice having them. They just smile at you. You put the kids to bed, but still they're hanging around. Finally you strip down to your underwear and lie down on the couch until they realize that maybe it's time to put on their coats and think about heading home.

I could go on about the conditions and limitations on my love. But Jesus is another story. Scripture says He loves all kinds of people—even the ones who are "impossible" to love. He loves us—purposefully, passionately, unconditionally.

Let's look again at this well-known passage from Romans:

> I am convinced that nothing can ever separate us from God's love. Neither death nor life, neither angels nor demons, neither our fears for today nor our worries about tomorrow—not even the powers of hell can separate us from God's love. No power in the sky above or in the earth below—indeed, nothing in all creation will ever be able to separate us from the love of God that is revealed in Christ Jesus our Lord.
>
> ROMANS 8:38-39

The kind of love expressed in this passage is far beyond human love. Nothing can make it fade or fail. Nothing can hold it back—not even the things we've done. God loves us . . . without condition.

This reality came crashing into my understanding in a new way a few years ago after an incident that happened with my daughter.

Since Charisse was about six months old, I've made it a weekly habit to allow Lucretia to sleep in while I take care of our daughter. I get my daughter out of bed, get her dressed, and take her on a breakfast date.

One particular morning I opened the door to walk into Charisse's room, and the smell that met me just about knocked me cold. I said out loud, "What in the heck is going on?"

When I walked around the corner and looked into my daughter's bed, the mysterious smell was a mystery no more—she was sitting in about an inch of vomit. I'm sorry, I know that's gross. But at least you're reading about it and didn't have to be there. You can take my word for it: the sight and smell were absolutely awful.

I stood there for a second or two trying to figure out what to do. Honestly, part of me wanted to scream for my wife to rescue me. (I know, typical man!) However, at that moment, Charisse reached out both arms toward me and simply said, "Daddy."

Let me ask you a question: how do you think I responded?

Did I yell at her for making such a mess?

Did I tell her to clean up the mess and I'd be back later to see how she'd done?

Did I lecture her for not getting out of bed and hitting the toilet?

No! I immediately picked her up, held her close, and told her everything was going to be all right. Then I put her in the bathtub and cleaned her up. Afterward I cleaned the sheets and her entire bedroom. Why? It's quite simple—because my love for her is based not on her performance but on her position as my daughter. No mess she could ever make would stop me from loving her.

I know the struggle you may be having right now. You want to believe God loves you this way, but you just can't seem to let go of what you did—or maybe what was done to you.

But here's the truth: what has defeated us in our past does not have to define who we are.

Breaking free

Let's think about the giant Goliath again. Even though he was the biggest, most intimidating force the Israelites had ever seen, he was brought down by a simple stone.

It's funny to think it was a stone that brought the giant down, because many generations after David, a stone was a symbol of freedom once again.

Two thousand years ago, a stone was rolled in front of a tomb, and everyone thought the Son of God was dead forever, His ministry was over. However, three days later, the stone was rolled away, sealing the deal that Jesus Christ had been raised from the dead. Now everyone who belongs to Him can live in the victory He has provided.

I may not be the person I need to be, but I am not the person I used to be. Jesus Christ has set me free from the prison of the past, and He can do the same for you.

Only when we understand that Christ paid for our sin and wants us to break free from its guilt and pain will we truly begin to live a life that is unleashed.

CHAPTER 4

THE GREAT AMERICAN LIE

I'll bet you've never heard of snow snakes! I hadn't either . . . until I was four years old and my father gave me a warning about these frightful creatures.

I grew up in South Carolina, and once every two or three years we get what I would call a pretty decent snowfall (decent meaning two or three inches). When this happened, people would lose their minds and purchase ridiculous amounts of bread and milk in the fear that the grocery stores might shut down for weeks (which has never happened).

One morning I awoke to discover there had been a significant snowfall the night before. I was out of my mind with excitement! I leaped out of bed and bundled up so I could head outside and play. But then came the bad news: my father told me no.

I informed my father that I was going outside anyway.

He shrugged his shoulders. "Okay, that's fine," he said. "But be careful—there are snow snakes out there!"

We need to pause here for a moment: I was—and am—absolutely terrified of snakes of any kind. I know there are people who claim that there are "good snakes," but I say the only good snake is a dead one! My dad knew that if there were snakes involved, I would do pretty much anything he told me to do.

But even at four years old I had my doubts about snow snakes. So I tested the waters a bit: "There are no such things as snow snakes," I said to my dad.

"Yes, there are," he told me. "They're real, and they only come out when it snows."

That was all it took to convince me. I don't know how it is with you, but when I was a kid, if my dad said something and then assured me it was true, I believed him. But I was still pretty curious about these creatures, so I asked, "Well, do they bite you?"

"Nope," my dad said. "They jump up your butt and freeze you to death!"

I was truly horrified now. This thought was more than I could bear. I stayed inside for the rest of the day.

A day or two later the snow melted, and I went back to the Christian preschool I was attending. The teacher asked, "How many of you boys and girls went outside and played in the snow?"

All the students raised their hands . . . except me.

"Perry, you didn't go outside and play in the snow?" she asked.

"No, ma'am," I replied.

"Why not?"

"Well, because I was scared of the snow snakes," I said.

"Perry, there's no such a thing as snow snakes."

"Yes, ma'am, my daddy told me there are!"

Then she asked with a smile, "Well, do they bite you?"

Needless to say, I had to visit the principal's office (in preschool, no less) after reporting to her how snow snakes strike their prey.

This story is now part of our family lore, but I think it also proves a point beyond that. Believing lies often holds us hostage and prevents us from living the life we are called to live. When I bought the story about the snow snakes, my fear caused me not only to stay inside but also to spread the lie to others at school.

Unfortunately, I see so many Christians doing the same thing. They believe lies about God—lies that hold them captive in the prison of religion. Then they turn around and pass on those lies to others.

One of the biggest lies we believe in this culture is what I refer to as "the Great American Lie."

Now before I expose this falsehood, I must warn you that you're likely going to get angry with me, because this is something many people desperately want to believe. It's a lie parents and teachers pass on to children every day. Hundreds—maybe even thousands—of books have been written that endorse this lie, and it's rampant in movies and online.

Here it is: You can do anything you want to do and be anything you want to be if you just believe in yourself and try hard enough.

So many people have bought into that lie hook, line, and sinker. But I need to tell you something: it's simply not true.

Let me share some personal examples.

I am about six feet six inches tall, and I weigh around 225 pounds. With that information in mind, what if I told you I really wanted to be a jockey and it was my dream to ride the winning horse in the Kentucky Derby? Be honest—you'd probably laugh a little and say, "Dude, at your size, the horse might actually try to ride you."

I am not the size, shape, or weight needed to be a successful jockey. No matter how much I believed in myself and no matter how hard I tried, I would only wind up feeling like a failure. I'd be a fool to dedicate my life to something I was obviously not created to do.

Well, then, what about *American Idol*?

I admit that *American Idol* has brought attention to some amazing talent and has helped launch the careers of several singers who probably would have gone unnoticed otherwise. But I hardly ever watch the final episodes. Why? Because honestly I get much more entertainment out of the early shows, when people are auditioning. And it's not because I like to recognize raw talent. Rather, I enjoy watching the people who stroll in to the audition, hold their heads high, announce what they're going to sing, and then. . . . Let's just say I've heard cows dying in hailstorms that sounded better than what comes out of their mouths.

I've heard people ask, "Why in the world would someone like that audition? Why would they think they had a chance?" But in my mind it's pretty simple: they have bought into the Great American Lie. At some point someone told these people that if they believed in themselves and tried really hard, they could be great singers and go on to have record-breaking careers. So they went on *American Idol* and made fools of themselves in front of the entire watching world.

In case I haven't been blunt enough already, let me say it one more time: the idea that you can do anything and be anything if you just believe in yourself is a lie. And if you believe this lie, it's only going to lead to disappointment and frustration.

So what's the truth? If I can't do anything I want to do and be anyone I want to be, then why in the world am I on this big ball of dirt called Earth? I would say that's a fair question. And if we're willing to embrace the answer, it can have unleashing power in our lives.

The true reason we're here is that God created us on purpose, with a purpose, and for a purpose. We are *not* accidents. The key to living a meaningful life is to focus not on what we want but rather on who Jesus is and what He wants for us. As we wrap ourselves up in Him, we find more purpose, meaning, and joy than we ever could have imagined.

In this chapter I want to challenge you to ask yourself two questions to help you move beyond your vision for your life and toward God's vision for you. Are you ready to dig deep?

The key to living a meaningful life is to focus not on what we want but rather on who Jesus is and what He wants for us.

QUESTION #1: Do you believe God wants to do more in your life than you can imagine?

Ephesians 3:20 says that God "is able to do immeasurably more than all we ask or imagine, according to his power that is at work within us" (NIV).

I believe every verse in the Bible is important; however, there are certain verses that seem to set my soul on fire and capture my imagination. I call these "life verses" because they have made such a significant impact on the way I think and act.

This passage from Ephesians is one of my life verses—something I've hung on to through the ups and downs as I've followed Christ. My life is far from perfect, but I can honestly say that God has blessed my life beyond what I could ever have imagined. My wife, my little girl, the church I serve, the friends I have, and even the fact that I was able to graduate from college are all results of God's work in my life.

At this point you might be feeling skeptical—maybe you even want to throw this book across the room. *Well, that's awesome for you,* you might be thinking. *I'm glad your life is going so well, but, dude, mine stinks.*

Because of what you've gone through, you believe God has forgotten you or abandoned you or simply doesn't care about you.

If so, my prayer is that you would be encouraged. Even though you may feel as if you are in the "valley of the shadow of death," God is the author of your life. He can take your pain and turn it into progress.

We would never say that a movie is bad because we don't like a section in the middle. Sure, there may be a scene or two that rub us the wrong way, but we have to wait to make our judgment until the movie is over.

The same is true of life: we have to choose not to allow what we're going through at the moment to define our entire view of God. Your life isn't over yet. As long as you're breathing, there's still hope.

Let's pick up where we left off in 1 Samuel 16, where the prophet Samuel anointed David as the king. When Samuel arrived in Bethlehem, Jesse called for all his sons except David to see who might be the next leader of Israel. None of these brothers were chosen.

Meanwhile, David—the one *not* invited to the anointing party—was hanging out with the sheep in the middle of a field somewhere. He was at the bottom of the list of brothers and was overlooked by those closest to him. Yet at that very moment God was working behind the scenes, making preparations for this forgotten shepherd boy to be one of the greatest leaders the world has ever known.

Let me stop right here and say that what was true of David is true of you if you are in Christ. We can't always see God at work, but Jesus said He's always working (see John 5:17). And believe it or not, your heavenly Father has been at work behind the scenes on *your* behalf. Even if you feel unimportant or overlooked, know that God sees you and has specifically chosen you.

Now back to our story. . . . David was finally summoned to the party. I picture the older brothers sort of rolling their eyes and giving one another looks that communicated, "Whatever." Then something pretty incredible happened.

> Jesse sent for [David]. He was dark and handsome, with beautiful eyes.
>
> And the LORD said, "This is the one; anoint him."
>
> So as David stood there among his brothers, Samuel took the flask of olive oil he had brought and anointed David with the oil. And the Spirit of the LORD came powerfully upon David from that day on. Then Samuel returned to Ramah.
>
> 1 SAMUEL 16:12-13

Did you catch that? David was anointed. Whoa! That's something we don't have much context for in our culture, but in David's day it was a pretty big deal. Here's what would typically happen: a priest (or, in this situation, a prophet) would perform a sacred ritual by pouring a flask of oil on a person's head. Anytime someone was anointed in the Old Testament, it was symbolic of God's choice. It meant that He had a significant task for that person to do and that He would empower him or her to do it.

In David's case, God had called him out of a life of obscurity and a seeming lack of purpose and chosen him to do something that no doubt blew his mind.

Scripture makes it clear that God has a habit of taking average, ordinary people and using them to accomplish extraordinary things.

Take Gideon, for example. He was in a winepress, hiding from his enemies and full of doubt about what God was calling him to do (see Judges 6). Yet God used him to lead an army and free the nation of Israel from bondage.

The apostle Peter denied Christ and even called down curses

on himself when Jesus was in His darkest hour. Yet after Jesus' resurrection, God used Peter to deliver a message that led to three thousand people receiving Christ (see Matthew 26; Acts 2).

The apostle Paul had quite a nasty habit of murdering Christians. Yet God transformed him into one of the most effective pastors and missionaries the world has ever seen (see Acts 9).

For some reason it isn't hard to believe God had great plans for David. And for many of us it isn't hard to believe God has great plans for other people. But when it becomes personal, we get a little antsy. "*Me*?" you ask. "Really?"

But David wasn't the only one who was anointed. In this era after Christ's death and resurrection, it's not just kings and priests who are anointed but everyone who receives Christ. We read about it in Ephesians 1:13-14 (NIV, 1984):

> You also were included in Christ when you heard the word of truth, the gospel of your salvation. Having believed, you were marked in him with a seal, the promised Holy Spirit, who is a deposit guaranteeing our inheritance until the redemption of those who are God's possession—to the praise of his glory.

The Bible says that when we believe in Christ, we are marked with a seal—the Holy Spirit. What anointing oil did in the Old Testament to set people apart as chosen, the Holy Spirit does in the New Testament. What was true of David thousands of years ago is true of us right now: God has created us on purpose, with a purpose, and for a purpose. He has clearly identified us as His for the whole world to see.

One of my greatest fears when I travel is being separated from my luggage—either as a result of losing it or as a result of having it stolen. I get nervous every time I'm in the baggage-claim section of an airport, and I can't calm down until I have my luggage in my hand.

One year a friend bought me a nice black suitcase as a gift. It had plenty of room inside, and I could tell right away it would be ideal for travel.

But on my first trip I discovered one problem: there are approximately 1,283,487 black suitcases on every airplane. So when the luggage was being unloaded onto the conveyor belt, I thought every big black suitcase was mine.

This went on for a year or so, as I continued to agonize over not being able to identify my suitcase. Then one night Lucretia was wrapping presents, and she had some gold ribbon in our living room.

I leaped to my feet, seized the black suitcase from our bedroom, and brought it into the living room. I then took the gold ribbon and wrapped it around every handle on my suitcase. (I think I might have overdone it, as I believe we had to go out and buy more ribbon.)

Now my suitcase wasn't the same as every other black suitcase. It was unique; it had a distinguishing feature that made it stand out. Now I was easily able to identify it as mine. I had marked it with a "seal," if you will.

That's what happens when we come into a relationship with Christ. He wraps us up in His unleashing grace. We are marked, set apart, unique. And He is able to accomplish far more than we could ever think or imagine—not because of who we are but because of whose we are.

What does God want for me?

One of the most common questions I've received in the nearly twenty years I've been doing ministry is, "How in the world do I know what God wants for my life?" What I've discovered along the way is that God wants us to know His will for us even more than many of us actually want to know it.

There are books you can read, tests you can take, and prayers you can pray to help you figure out your gifts and what God might be calling you to. But it doesn't have to be complicated. The best advice I can give you about how to discover what the Lord wants for you is simply to look at three factors.

FACTOR #1: YOUR OPPORTUNITIES

The apostle Paul tells us in Ephesians 5:15-16 that we should be wise and make the most of every opportunity.

I was the king of this in college.

Everyone who has ever watched a late-night television commercial knows that the snack attack, as I like to call it, can hit at any time. This often presented a problem for me because I was so broke in college that I had to go to Kentucky Fried Chicken to lick other people's fingers!

However, in the local mall there was a Chick-fil-A restaurant where a sweet old lady gave out samples of chicken every afternoon, usually between one o'clock and three o'clock. There may have been an occasion or two when the snack attack hit and I drove to the mall so I could walk by the lady a time or two—or eighteen—and satisfy my craving. I was simply making the most of an opportunity.

David never went out looking to become king—he didn't send out résumés or "network" with bigwigs to get his foot in the door. He simply walked through the doors God had opened for him. The opportunity just landed on his lap when he was off doing his ordinary job. Even after he was anointed king of Israel, we don't see him trying to convince others that he was gifted to be king. In fact, we see quite the opposite:

> One day Jesse said to David, "Take this basket of roasted grain and these ten loaves of bread, and carry them quickly to your brothers. And give these ten cuts of cheese to their captain. See how your brothers are getting along, and bring back a report on how they are doing." David's brothers were with Saul and the Israelite army at the valley of Elah, fighting against the Philistines.
>
> 1 SAMUEL 17:17-19

This passage shows David as an incredible example of both humility and a willingness to seize an opportunity placed in front of him.

David's father asked him to run an errand—to take some bread to his brothers. What if David had said, "Look, Dad. I'm sorry, but there has been a misunderstanding. See, I've been named the future king, so I don't do errands anymore. Seriously, Pops, don't you recognize me? I had oil poured on my head! I am anointed! I'm way too important to be delivering bakery items. Now, if you would be so kind as to apologize, I might allow you to live in my palace one day."

If David had thought he was too good for this task, he would have missed the opportunity God had planned for him. The way for him to discover his gift wasn't to convince himself and other people how gifted he was. Instead, he found his calling simply by embracing what God placed right in front of him.

In 1 Samuel 17:20 we see David doing just that:

> David left the sheep with another shepherd and set out early the next morning with the gifts, as Jesse had directed him. He arrived at the camp just as the Israelite army was leaving for the battlefield with shouts and battle cries.

Before I move on, let me say that if God has gifted you to do something, you will not have to tell anyone. Does LeBron James have to convince us that he is gifted to play basketball? No, he simply plays the game, and his gift is obvious. Does Justin Bieber have to boast about what a talented singer he is? No way—he just sings, and everyone becomes aware of his gifting.

David knew he was called and gifted, yet he chose to humble himself and make the most of the opportunities he was given. We will never become fully who God has called us to be unless we grasp that life is not about getting other people to serve us but about how we can serve others.

I would also venture to make this point: David would never have been aware of the opportunity to fight and ultimately get victory over Goliath had he not embraced the seemingly small opportunity to take some bread to his brothers. Often the key to tremendous breakthroughs in our lives is our willingness to take the small steps behind the scenes.

FACTOR #2: YOUR OBSESSIONS

We live in a world that is obsessed with the meaningless and the temporary. Let me give you an example.

In the 1980s there was a music group called New Kids on the Block. You may remember them. In fact, you may even have had New Kids bed sheets—admit it! If you haven't heard of the New Kids, take my word that gobs of people—mostly young females—were absolutely obsessed with them at the time. However, after several years, they sort of faded into obscurity. What was once a nationwide sensation was soon forgotten.

Then in the 1990s along came a band called Hanson, and the world went crazy over them too. People bought their music by the truckload, and their concerts were some of the hottest tickets out there. But today . . . well, I've got to be honest: I just don't hear much about them anymore.

We will all find ourselves obsessed with something—it's just part of the way we're wired. It's not a question of if we'll be obsessed with something but of *what* our obsession will be. So the question each of us needs to ask when we consider God's plan for our lives is this: What am I obsessed with that actually matters when it comes to an abundant and eternal life?

Let's continue digging into the story about David:

> The Israelite and Philistine forces stood facing each other, army against army. David left his things with the keeper of supplies and hurried out to the ranks to greet his brothers. As he was talking with them, Goliath, the Philistine champion from Gath, came out from the Philistine ranks. Then David heard him shout his usual taunt to the army of Israel.
>
> As soon as the Israelite army saw him, they began to run away in fright. "Have you seen the giant?" the men asked. "He comes out each day to defy Israel. The king has offered a huge reward to anyone who kills him. He will give that man one of his daughters for a wife, and the man's entire family will be exempted from paying taxes!"
>
> David asked the soldiers standing nearby, "What will a man get for killing this Philistine and ending his defiance of Israel? Who is this pagan Philistine anyway, that he is allowed to defy the armies of the living God?"
>
> 1 SAMUEL 17:21-26

We see from David's questions at the end of this passage that he was fired up by the entire scene. Who is this giant? How dare he taunt God's people like that? And why are the Israelites running in fear when they should be facing this guy in faith? David couldn't just sit by and do nothing. A fire developed deep inside him, and he became obsessed with taking on this giant.

What is it that absolutely stirs a fire inside you? What riles you up so much that you think, *Someone has got to do something about that!* I'll let you in on a little secret—the reason you're seeing something that bothers you is not so you can simply share the *information* with others but so you can be a part of the *transformation* God wants to do through you.

In other words, maybe it's time for you to stop complaining about what bothers you and actually do something about it.

In 1996 God put a desire in me to start a church. As I surveyed church culture in this country, I realized that most churches aren't designed to reach the lost but rather to cater to the needs of a few and to keep certain people happy. It bothered me—it literally kept me up at night. Over the next several months I became obsessed over this idea (my wife might say "obsessed" is an understatement). Finally, in 1999, with no job, no health insurance, and no idea what we were doing, Lucretia and I made the decision that instead of just being bothered by something, I was going to attempt to do something about it.

So what is it? What is that one thing that's wrong in the world that lights a fire under you and makes you feel as if someone should do something about it?

Maybe you feel a tug toward overseas ministry. If so, take a short-term trip to see if God uses that experience to set your heart on fire.

Maybe you have a heart for single mothers. If so, find a woman who needs help and watch her children for free once a week so she can run some errands.

Maybe you care about senior citizens in your community who

are struggling. If so, volunteer to help them with yard work on a Saturday afternoon.

What are your obsessions—those things that in the grand scheme of eternity really do matter? Finding the answer to that question will get you one step closer to finding your true purpose.

FACTOR #3: YOUR OPPOSITION

You might be surprised to see opposition listed as one of the ways to determine your calling. But please understand this: it is a spiritual impossibility to embrace all that God has for you and keep everyone in your life happy. And one other thing—you will be miserable if you try. If people crucified Jesus for following God's plan for His life, then you and I can't expect obedience to be a day at a theme park.

David was bothered by the scene with Goliath. His heart was inflamed, and he was full of desire to do something. Then we see what happens in 1 Samuel 17:28:

> When David's oldest brother, Eliab, heard David talking to the men, he was angry. "What are you doing around here anyway?" he demanded. "What about those few sheep you're supposed to be taking care of? I know about your pride and deceit. You just want to see the battle!"

If you jumped into this story at this point, you might wonder who had peed in Eliab's cornflakes that morning. David is simply expressing what some have referred to as "holy discontent," and out of nowhere his older brother loses his mind.

But we need to note the context here. Eliab is most likely dealing with insecurity, jealousy, and fear. There's no doubt the scene from the previous chapter is fresh in his mind—that day he was passed over for kingship in favor of his baby brother, David. He was probably also dealing with the fact that he'd been just sitting at camp for forty days while Israel's enemies rubbed in the fact that they could intimidate and manipulate the army of God.

Eliab had decided long before this moment that he was going to complain about the problem but not actually do anything to solve it.

As a result, his attack on David quickly became personal. David understood that if he was going to step up and embrace the opportunity God had placed in front of him, he would have to do so in the face of opposition.

I love what Scripture says in Isaiah 54:17:

> No weapon turned against you will succeed.
> You will silence every voice raised up to accuse you.
> These benefits are enjoyed by the servants of the Lord;
> their vindication will come from me.
> I, the Lord, have spoken!

One of the things we must understand when reading this text is that the Bible doesn't promise there will not be weapons turned against us, but rather that none of the weapons turned against us will succeed. Those might be weapons of war, as they were for David, or they might be more subtle ones, such as gossip, slander, criticism, jealousy.

The apostle Paul puts it this way:

> I'm not trying to win the approval of people, but of God. If pleasing people were my goal, I would not be Christ's servant.
>
> GALATIANS 1:10

It is insane to believe that everyone is going to understand, embrace, and support what the Lord is calling us to. When we meet resistance, even from our own families, we need to keep pressing on to live the unleashed life God has planned for us. As followers of Christ, our primary goal is not to be understood but rather to be obedient.

As followers of Christ, our primary goal is not to be understood but rather to be obedient.

QUESTION #2: Why would you settle for a lesser vision than the one the Creator has for you?

Don't tell me that one person can't make a difference.

Our world has been turned upside down by individuals who were willing to follow big dreams.

Who would have guessed that Abraham Lincoln, a man from humble beginnings, would be used to end slavery and preserve the Union?

Or what about Martin Luther King Jr., who had a passion to see the racial lines destroyed?

Or William Wilberforce, who was committed to ending the slave trade in eighteenth- and nineteenth-century England?

I know your objections already. You're probably saying, "Perry, I will never give a speech on the mall in Washington, DC, or put an end to slavery. I'm just an average person."

You might be right, but some of the biggest difference makers are people who accomplish things behind the scenes—things we never see on this side of heaven.

Take my mother, for example. She never held a leadership position in a church, she never preached a sermon, and as far as I know, she never set foot in a college class. However, God used her in a significant way to make a difference in the life of at least one person: me.

I can honestly say that I'm the man I am today and I'm doing the things I'm doing because of her. She knew God had a purpose for her life, and she embraced her role as a mother with her whole heart. I can remember walking into the kitchen every morning and seeing her with an open Bible and a cup of coffee, trying to discern God's voice.

Because of my mother's influence, I now follow Christ too. I'm also bringing up my daughter to know Him, and I'm trying to lead a church to follow Him too.

If God, the Creator of the universe, created us on purpose, with a purpose, and for a purpose, then why in the world would we be willing to settle for anything less?

If God, the Creator of the universe, created us on purpose, with a purpose, and for a purpose, then why in the world would we be willing to settle for anything less?

One of my favorite authors, C. S. Lewis, says in *The Weight of Glory*, "If we consider the unblushing promises of reward and the staggering nature of the rewards promised in the Gospels, it would seem that Our Lord finds our desires not too strong, but too weak. We are half-hearted creatures, fooling about with drink and sex and ambition when infinite joy is offered us, like an ignorant child who wants to go on making mud pies in a slum because he cannot imagine what is meant by an offer of a holiday at the sea. We are far too easily pleased!"

So what's holding you back? Becoming the person God has called you to be begins where you are right now, not after you become some future version of yourself.

It's time to stop making excuses. God hasn't called us to make excuses; He has called us to make a difference. And people who make excuses never make a difference.

Stop saying you're too young. God used John the Baptist when he was still in the womb (see Luke 1:39-45); He called Samuel into the ministry when he was still a young boy (see 1 Samuel 3); and most scholars believe David was a teenager when he faced Goliath (see 1 Samuel 17).

Stop saying you are too old. The Bible says that Moses was eighty years old when God called him to lead a major relocation project (see Exodus 7:7), and Noah was around five hundred years old when God told him to build the ark (see Genesis 5:32–6:22)!

God hasn't called us to make excuses; He has called us to make a difference.

Stop saying you've messed up too much to be used by God. Scripture is full of imperfect people who embraced the love of a perfect God and then went on to make an impact for His Kingdom. Elijah wanted to quit. Jonah ran from God. Thomas doubted the resurrection. And God did big things through them anyway.

Stop saying you're afraid of being uncomfortable. Jesus said that if we are going to be His followers, we have to take up our cross, not our mattress.

Stop saying you're uncertain of what may happen. David was willing to step into the valley to face Goliath that day with no guarantee he would be victorious. Think about it—nowhere in Scripture do we read that God told David he was going to win. David just saw an opportunity that he would rather have died than pass up, and he seized it.

Let's say you're walking down the street and come upon a beggar, and he convinces you to let him borrow a dollar. During the conversation you feel a tug of compassion for him, so you give him your telephone number and tell him to call you if he needs help again. Later that evening, you are awakened by a phone call. It's the beggar, thanking you for your generosity and telling you that he purchased you a gift.

What would your response be? Would you leap out of bed, get dressed, and try to find this guy? Or would you simply dismiss it because you know the guy didn't have anything significant to give? You would most likely thank him and then make a mental note to change your phone number the next day.

But what if you are at a dinner party and meet Bill Gates? Let's say he shows an interest in your business or ministry, and at the end of the conversation he asks for your card. The next morning you are awakened by a phone call, and on the other end of the line is someone who represents Bill Gates. This person tells you that Bill wants to give you a gift that is larger than any gift he has ever given to a person or corporation.

What would your response be to such an offer? I don't know about you, but I would cancel a kidney operation to get that gift. Why? While what the beggar has to give is most likely the result of what I gave him, Bill Gates has far more than I do and is capable of showering me with something I could never afford myself.

It's sad really—many of us would believe Bill Gates might make an offer like that, but we have a hard time believing the same thing about God.

God has infinitely more resources than Bill Gates—or anyone else on earth, for that matter. God says in Psalm 50:10, "All the animals of the forest are mine, and I own the cattle on a thousand hills." And He doesn't just keep the treasures of the universe to Himself—He wants to share them with His children: "God will generously provide all you need" (2 Corinthians 9:8).

Once we know about the gifts God has generously poured out on us, we can't keep buying into the Great American Lie. He has a purpose for us that is so much fuller and richer than anything this world could offer. You are not an accident, and your life does have meaning. It's time to start paying attention to the opportunities, obsessions, and opposition that have been placed in your life so you can discover the unleashing power God has in store for you.

Let's go back to David for a second. He could have been a shepherd for the rest of his life, and I suppose he would have been a good one. Or he could have been a musician, since there's evidence he did that pretty well too. However, God created him to be a king—a ruler of the nation of Israel—and the way he discovered that was by following God's plan one step at a time. As he did so, his life was completely unleashed.

It started with a small step for David—taking the bread to his brothers. What's the next step for you?

CHAPTER 5

MOVING ON

How many speeding tickets have you received? Be honest!

Now here's my next question for you: were the tickets your fault? The reason I ask is because I personally have never received a speeding ticket that was my fault. It was just a simple misunderstanding (which none of the officers who pulled me over seemed to appreciate). And even the times I *was* going over the speed limit, I had some really good reasons why the posted speed limit should not apply to me.

In a few of those instances I had more important things to think about and wasn't paying attention to the speed limit, and in one case (okay, maybe two), I was simply comparing my speed to the speed of others around me. Still, there was a price to pay for not submitting to the law that had been clearly posted.

Despite my passionate pleas for mercy and my excellent explanations for why I had broken the law, I still received tickets that included fines for me to pay. And in each situation, I was delayed from making progress toward my ultimate destination.

The fact is, when we violate the standards that have been set, there is a price to pay.

Think of the physical standard of gravity, for example. I can claim that I don't believe in gravity. Maybe I've been wounded by it in the past, so now I think I'm an exception to its consequences. But even if I don't believe in it, the law of gravity still applies to me. If I go to the top of a building and jump off, all my previous assumptions about gravity will quickly change as I race toward the ground, screaming like a banshee!

No matter what I believe about gravity, I am still subject to its reality.

Just as there are physical standards (like gravity) and legal standards (like speeding tickets), there are spiritual standards as well. If we choose to ignore these standards or claim we are somehow exempt from them, we will ultimately pay the price.

Throughout my years in ministry, I've talked with a lot of people who felt as if they were being held back from the unleashed life God desires for them. I've come to the conclusion that one of our biggest barriers to spiritual breakthrough is the unwillingness to forgive others for the wrongs that have been done to us.

I know firsthand that offering forgiveness is hard to do. The emotions we feel as a result of wrongs that have been done to us are very real, and nothing we do seems to make them go away, no matter how much we pray or wish they wouldn't haunt us anymore. Since forgiveness is so hard, we decide our situation is somehow an exception to God's command to forgive. We don't grasp that when we refuse to forgive, we are actually holding ourselves back from living the unleashed life God desires for us.

As we return to David's story, let's pick up with the rather intense exchange between David and his brother Eliab right before David's battle with Goliath:

> When David's oldest brother, Eliab, heard David talking to the men, he was angry. "What are you doing around here anyway?" he demanded. "What about those few sheep you're supposed to be taking care of? I know about your pride and deceit. You just want to see the battle!"
>
> "What have I done now?" David replied. "I was only asking a question!" He walked over to some others and asked them the same thing and received the same answer.
>
> 1 SAMUEL 17:28-30

For years I read that part of the passage and skimmed over it, not comprehending its significance. But hang with me—this encounter with Eliab could have derailed David from going to the next level in his life.

I have a hunch there was some sibling rivalry in the family, and Eliab was holding on to some bitterness toward his little brother after David was chosen over him to be the next king of Israel. So when the opportunity presented itself, Eliab lashed out at David, attempting to publicly humiliate him.

And what was David's response? He didn't argue back. He didn't gather crowds of people to see who supported him and who supported Eliab. He didn't storm off, have a pity party, and lament all the hurt and pain Eliab had brought into his life.

He simply moved on.

While David could have been derailed from his calling at this moment and allowed a seed of anger to develop in his heart, he simply refused to allow it to take hold.

There is no record that after David had killed Goliath, he

came back to Eliab and addressed this issue with him. Later in David's life, when he was established as the leader of a group of warriors who were on the run from evil King Saul, David's brothers (including Eliab) rallied around him and followed his leadership (see 1 Samuel 22:1). And when David was crowned king over Israel, he didn't bring Eliab before him and say, "Hey, Bro, remember the time I was about to fight Goliath and you tried to put me down?"

David simply moved on and refused to allow unforgiveness to prevent him from becoming the person God desired him to be.

Forgiving others is something I've had to fight through myself. It hasn't been easy.

I was sexually molested twice before the age of ten. I put it in the back of my mind for years, but eventually it all came flooding back—what had been done to me and the resulting damage it did to my soul.

I wanted the offenders to suffer. I wanted them to come crying to me, admitting they were wrong and I was right. I had battles with them in my mind, and I relished those feeling of anger and bitterness for a while. But then I discovered that time does not heal all wounds—God does, over the course of time. As I walked more closely with Jesus and started to comprehend His complete forgiveness, it gradually became clear to me that in order to be like Him, I would need to offer that same forgiveness too.

Holding unforgiveness in my heart and expecting it to hurt my abusers was the equivalent of drinking poison myself and expecting it to kill the other guy. I thought I was punishing them, but in reality I wasn't doing any damage to them—I was only doing damage to my own soul and to my walk with Jesus.

My abusers weren't the only people I've had to forgive. I've had to learn this lesson over and over. No matter who you are or what your story is, I guarantee you're going to have to deal with people who have hurt you.

If you want to live a truly unleashed life, it is critical that you let go of any unforgiveness in your heart. Trust me—if you can get the forgiveness thing down, you will experience the kind of breakthrough you never imagined possible. It won't be easy. It will take prayer, guts, and a commitment to fight through the issues. But the Lord will give you the strength you need.

Here are three truths we need to understand when it comes to forgiveness.

TRUTH #1: Forgiven people forgive people.

Jesus had quite a bit to say about the topic of forgiveness—and specifically about forgiving others. Please notice that I didn't say that forgiven people *should* forgive people but rather that forgiven people *do* forgive. It's just a natural response—an outpouring of the same grace we ourselves have received.

Most of us are familiar with the Lord's Prayer. But have you ever studied Jesus' teaching that comes right after it in Scripture?

Let's take a look at Matthew 6:9-15:

Our Father in heaven,
    may your name be kept holy.
May your Kingdom come soon.
May your will be done on earth,
    as it is in heaven.
Give us today the food we need,
and forgive us our sins,
    as we have forgiven those who sin against us.
And don't let us yield to temptation,
    but rescue us from the evil one.

> If you forgive those who sin against you, your heavenly Father will forgive you. But if you refuse to forgive others, your Father will not forgive your sins.

Whew, that's intense! In my years as a pastor, a number of people have asked what I think that last part means, possibly hoping for some kind of loophole to soften Jesus' words. But I believe Jesus didn't mince words here; He said exactly what He meant. To put it bluntly, there is a price to pay for unforgiveness.

Some people might want to push back here and argue that this line of thinking falls into a works-based theology. And while it's true that we can't do anything to earn God's forgiveness, what Jesus is trying to point out is that it's a spiritual impossibility for a follower of Jesus Christ to hold on to anger, bitterness, and unforgiveness and not feel some sort of conviction and discomfort in doing so.

Let's put it another way: if you refuse to forgive, you will never experience the unleashing Jesus wants to do in and through you.

Jesus talks a lot about forgiveness in Matthew 18. As the scene unfolds, we see Peter, one of the twelve apostles, approach Jesus with a serious question.

> Peter came to [Jesus] and asked, "Lord, how often should I forgive someone who sins against me? Seven times?"
>
> MATTHEW 18:21

I've heard people interpret Peter's question as an attempt to impress Jesus. They speculate that he was showing off a graceful attitude to try to set himself apart in Jesus' eyes.

I think that's a bunch of bull!

I believe the reason Peter asked the question is that he was personally wrestling with the issue of forgiveness. Someone had hurt him at some point in the past, and he was having trouble moving on. In that verse I can feel the seriousness of his question, and maybe even a hint of frustration.

Did you know you aren't the first person on the planet to struggle with forgiveness? If Peter, one of the men who walked most closely with Jesus, wrestled with it, then there's no reason any of us should believe we'll be exempt.

There's no question: forgiveness is hard. I know you are probably thinking right now: Wait a minute—I've been seriously wounded. I've had something taken from me that I can never get back. God wouldn't ask me to forgive something this bad.

I would never want to downplay the real pain you've experienced. But I want you to be free. I want you to be able to fight through the chains of unforgiveness that hold you down.

It's interesting to note Peter's use of the number seven in his question. In Scripture, seven is commonly referred to as the number of completion. God took seven days to finish his creation, including a day of rest (see Genesis 1–2). The Passover celebration was to last for seven days (see Exodus 12). There are seven bowls of God's wrath described in the book of Revelation (see Revelation 16:1). Seven angels and seven trumpets will announce God's judgment in the last days (see Revelation 8). There are seven apostles. (Gotcha on the last one!)

So when Peter asked Jesus if he should forgive up to seven times, he was essentially asking, "Should I completely forgive people for the wrong that they've done to me?"

Jesus' reply no doubt shocked Peter:

> "No, not seven times," Jesus replied, "but seventy times seven!"
>
> MATTHEW 18:22

Whoa! Jesus was basically telling Peter, "Not only should you completely forgive, but you should *continually* forgive." Jesus knew forgiveness is not a one-time choice. Rather, it's a daily decision we need to make if we want to live lives that are fully unleashed.

Forgiveness is not a onetime choice. Rather, it's a daily decision we need to make.

Trust me, I know you can't just wake up one morning and say, "Well, that person hurt me, but I forgive them," and that's the end of it. Jesus doesn't appear with some sort of fairy dust and sprinkle it over us so we automatically see rainbows and unicorns.

For me, it hasn't been easy to let go of the sexual molestation I experienced. Every time I hear about something like that happening to a child, all the old emotions come flooding back into my mind.

The struggle to forgive is real and raw. It's a battle we have to fight continually if we're going to stay dedicated to Jesus and what He has taught us.

It is in those moments that we have to say, "I've forgiven that person for what he did to me, and right now I choose to forgive again instead of hold court in my mind." Forgiveness needs to be an ongoing attitude that guides our minds and our hearts.

And make no mistake about it—Jesus didn't say that we should forgive the minor offenses but that we're off the hook for the big things. He said we should continually and completely forgive others.

TRUTH #2: Unforgiveness is a slap in God's face.

If we as Christ's followers believe He has completely forgiven us, why would we expect that He would demand anything less of us?

After Peter asked Jesus this legitimate question about how many times to forgive, Jesus did what He so often did when faced with an intense theological issue. He told a story! (Who says Jesus was boring?)

He began the story like this:

> The kingdom of heaven is like a king who wanted to settle accounts with his servants. As he began the settlement, a man who owed him ten thousand talents was brought to him. Since he was not able to pay, the master ordered that he and his wife and his children and all that he had be sold to repay the debt.
>
> MATTHEW 18:23-25 (NIV, 1984)

There are two things I want to point out here as this story relates to our own lives. First, the King (God) wants to settle accounts with His servants (us). Someday every one of us will stand before God and give an account of the life we've lived.

That awareness will elicit either fear or joy in us. But know this: if we are in Christ, we can be completely forgiven, which means that when God asks us to give an account, Jesus will step in on our behalf. That's good news!

The second thing we need to understand is that forgiveness will be costly. When I was a new believer and came across this story, I thought, *What in the world is a talent?* Then I went about my business, never taking the time to investigate.

Can you imagine my surprise when I discovered in studying this text that it took about twenty years to earn *one* talent? So when Jesus said this man owed ten thousand talents, He was saying this dude had an enormous debt to pay off. When the crowd heard this, there had to have been a few gasps as people thought,

No way! How could he accumulate such a huge debt? He'll never be able to repay that much money—he's screwed!

Before we move on, it's imperative to understand that the man in the story represents us. We've racked up a sin debt that is so big, so daunting, we'd have no hope of making a dent in paying it back, even if we tried our whole lives to do so.

We all sin—every single one of us. And none of us had to be taught to sin. We were, as the Bible says, born that way.

In June 2007 my wife and I (mainly my wife) gave birth to a beautiful little girl we named Charisse. And believe it or not, I have never had to teach her how to sin. Ever! I never had to sit her down and say, "Charisse, when you are playing outside with your friends and the ball comes to you, you are sharing too much. I'm going to need you to take the ball, run inside, and refuse to play. And when people are mean to you, you are too nice back to them. Let me show you how to punch someone in the throat."

We were born into sin. And our sin has consequences.

Many times we fail to see the consequences of our sin against God because, to be quite honest, we have a small view of Him. But we need to realize that the greater the person we sin against, the greater the consequences.

For example, if we had a conversation today and you told me a lie, there probably wouldn't be many long-term significant consequences, other than the fact that I wouldn't be able to trust you. However, if you stood before a federal judge today and told a lie, you would likely spend some time in prison. That's because the judge holds a much greater position of authority than I do.

If you decided to hit me, there might be some consequences, depending on your size and strength and whether there were eyewitnesses. However, if you decided to smack the queen of England in the face, you would probably get shot. Why? Because the queen holds a much greater position of authority than I do.

So how does all this relate to God? When we sin, we are ultimately sinning against Him, slapping Him in the face. And I would venture to say that the consequences of such an act are much worse than what you'd face for anything you could do to a judge or the queen.

Jesus continued with His story:

> The servant fell on his knees before him. "Be patient with me," he begged, "and I will pay back everything."
>
> MATTHEW 18:26 (NIV, 1984)

When Jesus got to this part of the story, there must have been people in the crowd who were shaking their heads in disbelief. They knew there was no way this guy could ever pay back the ten thousand talents. The debt was obviously out of his reach.

But many of us are just as delusional about our sin as this guy was about his IOU. We buy into the lie that our good deeds will outweigh our bad ones. We think God will somehow accept us based on our performance because we managed to work off all the bad stuff.

Believing this would be like strolling down to the local burger joint and ordering a double cheeseburger, a large order of fries, an apple pie with ice cream, and a small diet soda and believing the diet drink would cancel out everything else. (Oh, how I wish that were true!)

We know this is ridiculous when it comes to physical things, yet so many people believe it when it comes to spiritual matters. The fact is, our sin is a huge debt—one we could never repay with any amount of good works.

But Jesus provided hope for all of us in Matthew 18:27 (NIV, 1984):

> The servant's master took pity on him, canceled the debt and let him go.

This verse fills me with awe because that's exactly what God did for me through His Son, Jesus Christ. He saw my condition and realized there was no way I could possibly repay Him for the wrong I've done. In response, He had mercy on me and sent His Son to die in my place for my sin so I could have a relationship with Him.

He did not partially forgive me.

He did not conditionally forgive me.

He completely forgave my debt—all ten thousand talents of it. And if you are in Christ, then He did the same for you! You are completely forgiven.

So what would you expect from someone who had just had his massive debt canceled? Celebration? Worship? Appreciation? Gratitude? Surprisingly, though, we see a much different reaction from the man in this story.

> When that servant went out, he found one of his fellow servants who owed him a hundred denarii. He grabbed him and began to choke him. "Pay back what you owe me!" he demanded.
>
> MATTHEW 18:28 (NIV, 1984)

What? Did you catch that?

Notice that after the guy left the presence of the king, he didn't just happen to run into someone at the supermarket who owed him money. Nope—after his unbelievable encounter with mercy, he intentionally sought out someone who owed him a mere fraction of what he'd just been forgiven.

Forgiveness doesn't come naturally. If we aren't careful, we'll do the same thing the guy in this story did—we'll accept forgiveness for our own huge debt and then turn around and hold a comparatively small violation over someone else's head.

Let's keep reading to find out what happened to the guy who received forgiveness but refused to extend it:

> His fellow servant fell to his knees and begged him, "Be patient with me, and I will pay you back."
>
> But he refused. Instead, he went off and had the man thrown into prison until he could pay the debt. When the other servants saw what had happened, they were greatly distressed and went and told their master everything that had happened.
>
> Then the master called the servant in. "You wicked servant," he said, "I canceled all that debt of yours because you begged me to. Shouldn't you have had mercy on your fellow servant just as I had on you?" In anger his master turned him over to the jailers to be tortured, until he should pay back all he owed.
>
> This is how my heavenly Father will treat each of you unless you forgive your brother from your heart.
>
> MATTHEW 18:29-35 (NIV, 1984)

Incredible! The man who owed him a few thousand bucks essentially said the same thing to him that he said to the king: "Be patient with me, and I will pay you back." But the guy refused to extend mercy.

Then the king showed up. Apparently the guy's unforgiveness was obvious to everyone. And what happened? The man who received forgiveness but refused to extend it was placed in prison.

Before we get angry with the king for placing this guy in prison, we need to realize that the king didn't actually put the guy there. Rather, the man's attitude and actions put him there. He was responsible for the prison he was in—and so are we if we hold on to anger and unforgiveness.

We can memorize Scripture, volunteer at church, pray for hours a day, and live the best life humanly possible, but if we refuse to forgive others, we will place ourselves in prison and never experience the unleashing that accompanies true forgiveness.

TRUTH #3: Forgiveness is the key to your freedom.

If you're feeling locked in prison right now, I want to let you in on a secret: *you* hold the key that will release you from that dark place. The key is called forgiveness.

In Jesus' parable, the unmerciful servant ended up in prison, which, the last time I checked, isn't a place where most people want to spend a lot of time. The irony is that he didn't have to go there at all. The outcome could have been completely different if he'd simply extended the same grace he'd just received.

You are pushing back—I know you are. You've held on to your anger and unforgiveness for a long time, and you wouldn't know how to act if you finally let go. I can imagine your protests: "But, Perry, you don't know what that person did to me!"

You are right—I don't know. And I would never try to diminish the legitimate hurt and pain that have been brought upon your life. However, though I don't know what has been done to you, I do know what was done to Jesus. He was falsely accused, lied about, put on trial, mocked, beaten, nailed to a cross, and ultimately murdered. He did this to pay for your sins and mine. Yet while He was being mistreated, He prayed for forgiveness for the people who were doing this to Him (see Luke 23:34).

Let me ask you a tough question: are you better than Jesus? If He is our model—if He is the one we follow—then we need to embrace His call to forgive . . . completely and continually.

How to forgive those who hurt you

Okay, so maybe you're convinced that you need to let go of the pain someone has caused you and move on. But as we've already established, forgiveness isn't easy. There's no surefire formula or quick checklist to make it a reality in your life. But the Bible does give us some insights on how to move forward in the process of forgiveness.

You have to deal with the hurt.

Let's go back to our story about the debtor. Keep in mind that the debt he had been forgiven was enormous—ten thousand talents, which translates to millions or possibly even billions of dollars today. Then he found a guy who owed him what would be equal to a few thousand dollars in our society.

It's important to note that Jesus didn't downplay the significance of the money that was owed to this man. I don't know about you, but if someone owes me a few thousand dollars, that's a legitimate debt, and I'm going to want my money back.

Whether it's a financial obligation or something that has been done against us, we can all think of something that makes us feel as if someone owes us.

In my case, that someone is Roy Petit. We were in Ms. Nalley's fourth grade class, and one day my friend Donnie Farmer and I got sent out of the classroom for a paddling. (I have no idea why I got the paddling—I was such a model student!)

As we headed back to class, Donnie and I were trying to laugh it off, and we started bragging about how tough we were. We strolled into the room with huge smiles on our faces and informed everyone that our punishment wasn't that bad—that it didn't even hurt.

A few minutes later, when Ms. Nalley came back into the

room, Roy raised his hand. She called on him and he told her, "Perry and Donnie said the paddling you gave them didn't hurt."

I'm not sure, but I believe fire was coming out of Ms. Nalley's eyes, and it would have consumed me if I'd been sitting closer to her. On that day Donnie and I received a "two-for-one special" in the paddling department—and the second one *did* hurt, as Ms. Nalley invited the principal to do the honors!

Needless to say, I was angry at Roy. He'd hurt me (or, more accurately, he'd caused my rear end to hurt). I wasn't just physically wounded—my pride also took a serious hit. In my fourth-grade mind, I saw this situation as being all his fault, and I wasn't about to let it go. For the rest of the year, I might have taken several opportunities to inflict some sort of bodily harm on him while we were on the playground.

Some of us are carrying around pain that is much more intense than anything a tattling fourth grader could inflict. Maybe you were molested or raped. Maybe you were betrayed by someone you thought you could trust. Maybe someone stole something from you or abandoned you just when you needed that person most. I don't know what your specific pain is, but I know we've all been hurt at some point in our lives.

And yet Jesus commands us to completely and continually forgive the people who have harmed us. I know from personal experience this is not easy to do. Everything in us resists forgiving others, because it feels unfair to just "let them off the hook." But real forgiveness doesn't mean others won't be held accountable for what they've done. It just means letting God

Real forgiveness doesn't mean others won't be held accountable for what they've done. It just means letting God exact His justice in His time instead of trying to take things into our own hands.

exact His justice in His time instead of trying to take things into our own hands.

If there is someone you need to forgive, today is the day to make that decision. No matter how you feel, it's time to release that person from the debt he or she owes you, just as Jesus released you from your debt to Him.

You have to deal with the desire to handle it yourself.
Personally this is where I struggle most when it comes to forgiving others. There are days when I feel as if God may need a hand—after all, He's busy operating an entire universe, and there are probably things that fall off His radar, right? And so, being the unbelievably generous person I am, I'm willing to take things into my own hands and help Him out.

Is there anyone else who'll admit to being guilty of the same thing? The world calls it revenge; the Bible calls it sin.

I've got to be honest here—there are some Scripture verses that I just don't like. Hold on . . . before you judge me, notice I didn't say there are parts of Scripture I don't agree with. I am committed to the inerrancy of the Bible. But there are times when I come across a passage of Scripture that makes me think, *I really wish God hadn't said that!*

Romans 12:17-18 is one example:

> Do not repay anyone evil for evil. Be careful to do what is right in the eyes of everybody. If it is possible, as far as it depends on you, live at peace with everyone. (NIV, 1984)

The Bible says to live at peace "as far as it depends on you." That means that how the other person reacts, what the other person says, or even if that person is alive or dead doesn't really matter when it comes to our responsibility to forgive and move on. The peace we're called to extend isn't up to the other person. It has everything to do with our own willingness to forgive.

In other words, we have to stop trying to handle things and completely surrender the situation to the Lord. We have to stop taking every opportunity to gossip about the person who hurt us. We have to stop secretly wishing something bad would happen to the one who mistreated us. We have to offer forgiveness . . . completely and continually.

So how do we let go of the urge to take things into our own hands and get revenge? It might look different depending on each person's unique situation. But one thing always holds true: before we can get right with someone else, we need to get right with God. Forgiveness is *not* a natural response, so in order for us to offer it to others who have hurt us, we need God's help. It's only when we ask Him to work on our hearts and allow us to see people as He sees them that we'll be equipped with the supernatural ability to forgive.

It's only when we ask God to work on our hearts and allow us to see people as He sees them that we'll be equipped with the supernatural ability to forgive.

After our hearts are right with God, we might have a conversation with the person who hurt us and tell them we forgive them and we aren't holding what they did against them anymore. If the person is deceased or we've lost contact with them or it wouldn't be safe to communicate with them, we might write a letter expressing how we feel and releasing them from the debt they've racked up against us. Depending on the circumstances, that letter might never be sent—it might be something we do simply for our own benefit.

I remember a friend once suggested that I sit down and write a letter to someone who had wounded me deeply. Honestly, at the time I would have rather set my head on fire and had someone put out the flames with a sledge hammer. But I wrote it. And it was one of the most unleashing things I've ever done in my life. I didn't send the letter—and I never will—but it was my way of letting go of the sin that had been done against me and surrendering it to God.

You have to deal with the desire to have it your way immediately.

Confession time: I am not the most patient man on the planet. I don't like long lines at restaurants; I have no tolerance for slow drivers in the passing lane; and it always bothers me when the checkout line next to me is moving faster than mine.

I want what I want, and I want it *now*!

Many times we have the same problem when it comes to forgiveness. Another one of those Bible verses I don't particularly like is Romans 12:19:

> Dear friends, never take revenge. Leave that to the righteous anger of God. For the Scriptures say,
>
> "I will take revenge;
> I will pay them back,"
> says the LORD.

The Bible clearly says that God will repay those who wrong His children. In fact, as angry as you may be about the hurt that has been brought on you or someone you love, there's someone who is even more outraged—God! He simply will not tolerate His children being mistreated. But there's something else we need to know about his justice: He may not bring it about in the way or the timing we request.

This hit me the other day when my four-year-old daughter told me some kids had been mean to her on the playground and said "bad things" about her. When I heard that, my blood pressure skyrocketed, and I wanted to know the kids' names, phone numbers, and addresses. My child had been hurt, and I wanted to make things right. Still, I didn't just show up at the playground the next day—I had a bigger picture of justice than my daughter did.

God is the same way. He gets righteously angry when anyone is picking on His children. But He doesn't necessarily zap the offender on the spot. We have to trust that He will make everything right in the end and accept that His ways are wiser than ours.

> Just as the heavens are higher than the earth,
> so my ways are higher than your ways
> and my thoughts higher than your thoughts.
>
> ISAIAH 55:9

Taking your foot off the brakes

A few weeks ago I took Charisse outside so she could ride her bicycle. Keep in mind that she's four, so she's still learning how to do this. There are several hills in our neighborhood, and whenever she'd start going down one of them, she'd get scared and hit the brakes about every three feet.

It was a little frustrating, to be honest. I would try to run beside her, but I had to stop my big self every few seconds. Finally I said, "Charisse, baby, quit hitting the brakes, and this will be a lot more fun."

"But, Daddy, I'm scared."

All of a sudden I had an idea. I told her to wait right there, and I walked in front of her for about ten steps. Then I turned around and said, "Charisse, look at me. Don't look anywhere else but right here at Daddy. Trust me—when you get here, I will catch you."

She did as I said, and I think she was going Mach 9 by the time she got to me. For the rest of the day she never hit the brakes. She screamed with joy and couldn't stop telling me how much fun she was having.

If you're holding on to bitterness and unforgiveness, then you might as well be hitting the brakes on the unleashed life. I believe God is telling us the same thing I told Charisse: "Fix your eyes on me. Trust me. Believe that I will take care of you. Stop hitting the brakes."

It's only when we let go of our hurt and release it to our heavenly Father that we will feel the thrill and freedom of the downhill ride.

CHAPTER 6

TRIUMPH OVER TRAGEDY

My mother died of cancer when I was twelve years old.

It was one of the most horrible things I've ever gone through.

I know everyone thinks highly of their mom, but Mama really was incredible. I came along pretty late in her life—she gave birth to me when she was thirty-nine years old. (I tell everyone I was a Sunday-afternoon-nap baby!)

My mother spoiled me rotten, and I was, without a doubt, a mama's boy. She washed my clothes, made my bed, cleaned my room, and cooked me just about anything I wanted. I was well taken care of.

She was also the primary spiritual influence in my life. There's no one else who so clearly modeled for me what it looks like to walk with Jesus.

She made it a point to raise her son to know God too. I tell people that I had a "drug problem" when I was a kid—my mama drug me to church on Sunday morning; she drug me to church on Sunday night; and she drug me to church any other time she heard a rumor it might be open.

When I was a kid, we were the all-American family. Both my parents had great jobs, and we lived in a nice house and had a few nice cars. I attended a private school, and from my perspective, life was about as awesome as it could have been.

Then Mama got sick.

One summer we were taking a cross-country trip from South Carolina to California, and on the way back, Mama began complaining of some pain in her abdomen.

She went to the doctor when we got home, and he told her it was her gallbladder. He assured her that the pain and discomfort could be taken care of through surgery, so she and my dad scheduled the operation for about a week later.

I still remember the morning she went in for surgery. I gave her a kiss, told her I loved her, and went to school as usual. I wasn't worried at all because everyone had told us that this was a routine procedure and everything was going to be fine.

No one saw it coming.

I walked into our house that day after school, and the living room was full of people—my grandmother, my uncle, a couple of aunts, and one of my sisters. I could tell my dad had been crying, which was something I'd never seen in my life.

I couldn't figure out what in the world was going on. Finally Dad said to the entire room, "Helen has cancer. The doctor told me that when he opened her up for her surgery, he found it was everywhere. It had already spread too much for anything to be done. She probably won't see another Christmas."

That was in August. Mama went to be with Jesus on November 17 of that same year.

My life was shattered. This wasn't supposed to happen. My

mom was a good lady—she read her Bible, she loved Jesus, and she went to church. Good people weren't supposed to get cancer and die. Good people weren't supposed to suffer. If you did the right things, God protected you from pain, right?

I was bitter toward God. He had the power to heal my mother—I'd heard about it in the church my mom had dragged me to. If we prayed to God, He would answer us. He could have taken away her cancer at any time, but He didn't. He let her suffer and die.

God didn't follow my plans; He didn't do what I asked. And I was mad at Him for it. Maybe you can relate.

You planned on the marriage; you didn't plan on your spouse leaving you.

You planned for the child; you didn't plan for the miscarriage.

You planned on the job; you didn't plan on being fired.

You planned to save yourself for marriage; you didn't plan on the rape.

You planned on your child's college experience; you didn't plan on attending your child's funeral.

So what do we do in situations like these? How are we supposed to respond when the proverbial bottom falls out and we're left feeling empty and confused?

I remember being told after my mother's death, "Don't ask questions. Just trust God." Uh, I don't know about you, but for me that's pretty much impossible. When you're in pain, canned phrases like that don't assist with the pain. And in my opinion, those kinds of statements are often made by people who are intimidated by the situation and don't know what else to say.

Questions are natural, especially in the face of tragedy. And one of the most common questions all of us ask at some point is "Why do bad things happen to good people?"

But perhaps that isn't the most pressing question after all. If we can grasp three fundamental truths, that question will fade into the background.

TRUTH #1: God is good.

Hold on! I can feel you pushing back right now. We've just been talking about bad things happening, about people's worlds falling apart, about dreams being shattered, and the first thing I bring up is the goodness of God? Really?

In my years as a pastor walking with people who are hurting, the argument I most often hear goes like this: "Well, if God is good, why did *this* happen?"

It's a fair question. But it raises an even deeper question: What is our faith built on? Is it determined by the facts in the Bible or by our feelings?

Let's take a look at Matthew 7:7-11 as we wrestle through that.

> Keep on asking, and you will receive what you ask for. Keep on seeking, and you will find. Keep on knocking, and the door will be opened to you. For everyone who asks, receives. Everyone who seeks, finds. And to everyone who knocks, the door will be opened.
>
> You parents—if your children ask for a loaf of bread, do you give them a stone instead? Or if they ask for a fish, do you give them a snake? Of course not! So if you sinful people know how to give good gifts to your children, how much more will your heavenly Father give good gifts to those who ask him.

Jesus posed some excellent questions in this text. First, He asked how many fathers, if their children asked for bread, would give them a stone. That sounds insane, right? Try to imagine this scene: a dad goes through the Burger King drive-through and orders a huge meal for himself. When his son pipes up from the passenger seat, "Hey, Dad, can I have a Whopper Jr.?" the father opens the car door, picks up a rock, and hands it to the boy, saying, "Nope, here's your dinner."

That dad would be arrested, prosecuted, and most likely have his parental rights terminated!

Then Jesus went on to ask another question: how many dads would give their children a snake if they asked for a fish? That's jacked up! Picture this: a dad and his son are sitting at Red Lobster and the boy says, "Daddy, can I have fish tonight?"

The father replies, "No, Son, I've got a surprise for you." Then he reaches under the table and throws a snake at the boy.

I think we'd all agree that dude would get the "bad dad" award!

Jesus said that if sinful earthly fathers wouldn't give cruel gifts to their kids, how much more would our heavenly Father not do that?

All of us have received a bad gift from someone at some point. You know what I mean—the kind that when you open the present you say, "You shouldn't have," and you really mean it. But Scripture is telling us that God cannot give bad gifts to His children.

Maybe you're disagreeing with me here because you've received what you'd consider a bad gift from God. Maybe it came in the form of a financial loss or the death of a loved one or an illness or a disaster. But before we go any further, all of us need to answer this question: are we going to allow circumstances to determine our belief in God, or are we going to allow our belief in God to reign over our circumstances?

Are we going to allow circumstances to determine our belief in God, or are we going to allow our belief in God to reign over our circumstances?

This question is important, because if we trust in God only as long as He makes sure we have money, our dog never gets sick, our car always starts, and our family is always disease free, we aren't actually committed to Christ. Rather, we're just hanging on to a conditional sort of faith that says, "I will love and acknowledge You as long as You do good things for me!"

Have you ever noticed how quick we are to blame God for the difficulties in our lives but how much we take for granted all the undeserved kindness He shows us?

I woke up in a climate-controlled house today . . . due to the goodness of God.

I have a closet full of clothes . . . due to the goodness of God.

I have options about what type of food to eat this evening . . . due to the goodness of God.

The Bible tells us that every good and perfect gift that we have in life comes from God (see James 1:17). That means everything—not just "spiritual" blessings but everything good in our lives—comes as a result of His kindness.

I often travel by plane, and I always chuckle a bit when they insist I keep my seat belt on. *I'm in a hollow metal tube that's traveling at over five hundred miles per hour at thirty thousand feet,* I think. *If this puppy falls out of the sky, this stupid seat belt isn't going to do a whole lot for me.*

I've seen my share of news stories about airplane crashes, and they're always disturbing. When a tragedy like this happens, a reporter often interviews someone who says something to this effect: "If God is good, how could He let this happen?"

It seems that God always gets the blame for disasters. But I often wonder, If God gets the blame for the airplane that crashed, why doesn't He get the praise for the thousands of planes that take off and land safely every day?

Let me say it again: God is good!

"But if God is good, why is this pain in my life?" you might ask.

There are no easy answers to this question, and I don't think we'll ever fully comprehend the whys in this life. But one thing I've learned about pain is that God often uses it to identify a problem that, if not dealt with, could hurt us even worse down the road—or possibly even destroy us. Sometimes God uses pain to bring something harmful to our attention so we can remove it from our lives. This isn't cruel at all but rather is an act of generous mercy.

Think about it this way: if a doctor identifies a tumor in me and produces a scalpel, saying we need to do surgery as soon as possible, is he mean and unjust? Or is he good because he cares enough about me to cut me open and remove the thing that could ultimately end my life?

Sometimes God uses pain to bring something harmful to our attention so we can remove it from our lives.

I know personally how hard it can be to see the goodness of God in the middle of suffering. My father recently died after a decade-long battle with Alzheimer's disease. It became brutal to spend time with him as his mind gradually fell apart, as there were days he didn't even know who I was and he wasn't able to tell me he loved me.

Even so, I know God is good.

One of the marks of a person who is living an unleashed life is that they can acknowledge the goodness of God even when they are experiencing hell on earth. One of the passages that brought me comfort while I watched my father waste away was Habakkuk 3:17-18:

Even though the fig trees have no blossoms,
and there are no grapes on the vines;

even though the olive crop fails,
and the fields lie empty and barren;
even though the flocks die in the fields,
and the cattle barns are empty,
yet I will rejoice in the LORD!
I will be joyful in the God of my salvation!

The prophet Habakkuk says in this text that even though everything seems to be falling apart and life is not turning out quite as expected, he will rejoice in the Lord and trust in Him to be his strength.

In other words, even in the midst of tragedy, God is still good!

TRUTH #2: God is all-powerful.

I am not all-powerful. And from time to time I am rudely reminded of that fact.

I recall a day when some friends and I were playing in the ocean and the waves were unusually large. I was standing with my back to the surf, facing my friends while, unbeknownst to me, a massive wave was building behind me.

Did my "friends" warn me? Nope!

When the wall of water slammed me to the ground, it felt as if I'd been hit by an NFL linebacker. I'm pretty sure my face was the first thing to hit the sand, and somewhere along the way my swim trunks wound up around my ankles. There I was in the ocean, half naked and gasping for breath . . . and utterly helpless.

I finally made it to the surface, and as soon as I caught my breath—*bam*, another wave hit me, and I was back on the ocean floor again.

It took me about a minute to get my bearings again (and get my swim trunks pulled up!). The waves had thrown me around like a rag doll, and I was powerless to stand against them. I experienced in a personal way that day the remarkable strength of the ocean. Yet the Bible says God is so strong He "gathers the waters of the sea into jars" (Psalm 33:7, NIV)!

His power is breathtaking.

There are countless stories in the Scriptures about how God alters nature, time, and circumstances—and He doesn't even break a sweat to do so.

In the book of Joshua we read about a fierce battle between the Israelites and their enemies. The Amorites were fierce opponents, but God made it clear that His people would have the victory—not because of their own expertise in battle but because the Lord would fight for them. He even went so far as to redirect the very laws of nature to do so.

> On the day the LORD gave the Israelites victory over the Amorites, Joshua prayed to the LORD in front of all the people of Israel. He said,
>
> "Let the sun stand still over Gibeon,
> and the moon over the valley of Aijalon."
>
> So the sun stood still and the moon stayed in place until the nation of Israel had defeated its enemies.
>
> JOSHUA 10:12-13

The God who gathers up the sea in a jar and can make the sun stand still in the sky is the same God who is in charge of our lives as well. If there is something that feels too big for you to handle, rest in the assurance that it's not too big for God.

TRUTH #3: Bad things happen.

Charisse and I were jumping on the trampoline the other day and I "double bounced" her. Keep in mind that I am about six feet six and weigh about 225 pounds; she is four years old and weighs forty pounds soaking wet. So when I double-bounced her, she took off like a rocket, and I wasn't sure if she'd ever come down. (I'm glad Lucretia was inside and didn't see it!)

When Charisse landed, she gave me the most serious look. "Daddy," she said, "please don't ever do that again!"

She was scared, but I knew there was no reason to be. Why? Because we have a safety net around our trampoline that pretty much guarantees you won't fall off.

We have the same desire for a safety net around our lives. We think God owes us a "sorrow-free guarantee" that nothing bad is ever going to happen to us or anyone we love.

The problem is that there is no promise like that anywhere in the Bible. In fact, for most people we read about who follow God, we see just the opposite.

Let's pick up our story with David as he tried to convince King Saul to let him fight Goliath:

> "I have been taking care of my father's sheep and goats," [David] said. "When a lion or a bear comes to steal a lamb from the flock, I go after it with a club and rescue the lamb from its mouth. If the animal turns on me, I catch it by the jaw and club it to death. I have done this to both lions and bears, and I'll do it to this pagan Philistine, too, for he has defied the armies of the living God! The Lord who rescued me from the claws of the lion and the bear will rescue me from this Philistine!"

> Saul finally consented. "All right, go ahead," he said. "And may the Lord be with you!"
>
> 1 SAMUEL 17:34-37

There's something striking about the challenges David faced over the course of his life. These difficulties (like fending off wild animals that came after his sheep) weren't punishments from God. They were the training ground for what God would call him to do in the future. As was the case in David's life, many times what we view as some sort of punishment from God is actually His way of preparing us for something far beyond what we can comprehend.

Many times what we view as some sort of punishment from God is actually His way of preparing us for something far beyond what we can comprehend.

Stay with me for a minute here. Are you an animal lover? I have friends who allow their dogs to sleep in their beds with them and take their dogs everywhere they travel. Their dogs watch television on their own TV and actually have favorite shows they enjoy!

My friends really love their dogs.

Most of us can relate to loving a cat or a dog, and yet even that devotion pales in comparison with the love a shepherd has for his sheep. Today it's hard for us to comprehend someone who loves sheep because, well, most of us don't actually know too many shepherds. However, we see that Scripture frequently uses the metaphor of God Himself as a shepherd and us as sheep (see Genesis 48:15; Psalm 23; Luke 15).

When the prophet Samuel came to anoint David as God's chosen king, David was most likely about eighteen years old, and at the time he was out tending sheep. If he'd had a Facebook account, his status would have been "Hanging with the sheep." If he'd been on Twitter, he probably would have tweeted, "Taking the sheep to a new place to get water."

He loved his sheep, and he would have done anything to protect them from harm and to prevent them from getting lost. We might not realize what a big deal one sheep was back then because we figure they could just run down to Wal-Mart and buy another one (that store sells everything, right?). But in David's day, if something happened to one of his sheep, it would have been considered a tragedy.

In the passage from 1 Samuel 17, David was telling Saul about times when lions or bears came to take one of his lambs.

This would have been a tragedy for a shepherd like David!

When faced with this situation, David had a choice about how he would react. He could have gotten bitter at God. He could have spent the rest of his life crying and asking why. He could have turned his back on God altogether and said, "If God really loved me, He wouldn't have allowed that tragedy to take place."

That's the approach a lot of people take when something terrible happens. In fact, it's the approach I took when my mother died. But that's not how David responded.

Let's take a look 1 Samuel 17:35 again:

> I go after it with a club and rescue the lamb from its mouth. If the animal turns on me, I catch it by the jaw and club it to death.

I don't know about you, but I scream like a girl and stand on a chair when there's a spider in my house. I can't imagine going after a lion.

David's response to tragedy is an example for all of us: he got up, punched the lion in the mouth, and took his sheep back! He refused to let tragedy identify him and instead chose to walk in the triumph God gave him.

If David had stayed in the sheep pen feeling sorry for himself, he never would have tasted victory over Goliath. When God allowed David's confrontation with the lion and the bear, God wasn't punishing David. He was preparing him to face Goliath.

Whatever tragedy you've experienced in your life, I know it's real. I know the pain is still there. I know there are questions that still linger in your mind. But please understand that even if you can't see it yet, God just may be using this situation to prepare you for something down the road.

You just need to walk out of the sheep pen! That's when God's power can be unleashed in your life.

No bad gifts

As I was growing up, I always knew that my mom was fully devoted to God. But I had no idea until after her death just what a significant legacy she'd left me.

After Mama died, I was told a story about something that happened the day I was born. Apparently, right after I was placed in her arms, she told my dad, "His name is Perry, and he's going to be my preacher."

My first thought after hearing that was, *Not only am I not going to be a preacher, but I'm never going back to church.*

God obviously had other plans.

From the time my mother passed away in 1982 until the fall of 1989, I ran from God. I allowed the tragedy of her death to define me, and I even used her death as an excuse for my bad behavior.

Finally, after my senior year of high school, a friend of mine convinced me to go to church with him. I went one Sunday, and then again, and soon became a frequent attender. As I heard God's Word taught, something started to happen in my heart.

Finally, in May 1990, I surrendered my life to Jesus. I asked

Him to come in and take over my life, and when I did, He began to heal my heart. As I look back over the course of my life, I can honestly say that my mother's death was both a God thing and a good thing. I never would have believed it in the midst of my grief, but I discovered that God is a good God and He can't give bad gifts to His children.

Will I allow tragedy to cause me to live in self-pity or in triumph? Will I choose to live as a victim of what has happened to me, or will I walk in the victory Jesus has promised to those who follow Him?

I still don't understand all the whys, and I never really got my questions answered. But I did finally see that God is God and that He is all-powerful and good even when bad things happen. The question is, Will I allow tragedy to cause me to live in self-pity or in triumph? Will my difficulties cause me to shut down, or will they spark me to live an unleashed life? Will I choose to live as a victim of what has happened to me, or will I walk in the victory Jesus has promised to those who follow Him?

My mother's legacy lives on. Every morning I get out of bed, get a cup of coffee, and open my Bible . . . just as my mother used to do. Her death was not a tragedy but rather a triumph, as her prayers for me were answered. I am in ministry, just as she envisioned, and I am living for Jesus.

And one day all things will be made right and new when I see her on the other side of eternity. I will hold her hand, and together we will worship our Lord—the one who can take a tragedy and turn it into triumph.

CHAPTER 7

MORE THAN WE CAN HANDLE?

A man should never wear a Speedo. Ever!

I used to express that sentiment quite often and would defend it almost to the point of violence.

The reason, quite simply, was that every man I'd ever seen wearing one really shouldn't have been. I was firmly convinced that it just wasn't a good idea. Besides, I knew I, for one, would never wear one.

Until I attempted to run the Rock 'n' Roll Marathon in San Diego several years ago.

I was about fifteen or so miles into the race and slowing down when a dude passed me wearing nothing but a Speedo and a sombrero. And, just being honest, the guy was absolutely shredded. I think he probably had about negative 2 percent body fat, and he obviously spent about five hours a day lifting small cars.

I remember thinking when he ran by me, *Okay, so I'm wrong. That guy can wear a Speedo. In fact, if I looked like that, I'd probably wear one on a daily basis!*

There really is a connection here—I promise! My point is that I had a belief I thought was solid until I saw something (in this case, someone) that radically changed my mind.

Having served in ministry for more than two decades now, I've seen a common idea that simply isn't true dominate the landscape of the church. And in my opinion, it's one of the most damaging beliefs a Christian can hold.

I used to believe this idea myself. I spread it to other people. Shoot, I'm quite sure I even preached messages promoting this misguided belief. That is, until I began to look at my own life and the lives of those around me and began a serious study of what the Bible had to say about this. It didn't take long for me to discover that the idea is false. It leads to confusion and frustration, and it prevents people from living the unleashed life that God wants for them.

Here's the false idea: "God will never give you more than you can handle."

I suspect we've all had this concept pitched to us at some point as one of the key principles of the faith. We've heard it from the lips of other Christians; we've read books about it; we've seen the phrase on bumper stickers. But I'm telling you, it simply doesn't ring true—from the standpoint of human experience or from God's Word. When we buy into this false idea, it only leaves us confused, frustrated, and angry. And ultimately, after God does hand us more than we can handle, we may end up walking away from Him.

The truth is, God often allows us to face more than we can handle. But it's not because He's cruel or heartless. It's so we'll stop trying to live life on our own strength and learn to depend on His!

Before we go on, I want to acknowledge where this idea that God won't give us more than we can handle might have originated. The apostle Paul writes:

> The temptations in your life are no different from what others experience. And God is faithful. He will not allow the temptation to be more than you can stand. When you are tempted, he will show you a way out so that you can endure.
>
> 1 CORINTHIANS 10:13

This verse is a wonderful reminder of God's faithfulness—an assurance that He has our backs when we're tempted. But it doesn't say anything about God never giving us more than we can handle, as some people have interpreted it to mean. In fact, it was Paul who also wrote these words:

> We think you ought to know, dear brothers and sisters, about the trouble we went through in the province of Asia. We were crushed and overwhelmed beyond our ability to endure, and we thought we would never live through it. In fact, we expected to die. But as a result, we stopped relying on ourselves and learned to rely only on God, who raises the dead. And he did rescue us from mortal danger, and he will rescue us again. We have placed our confidence in him, and he will continue to rescue us.
>
> 2 CORINTHIANS 1:8-10

Wow! Here's one of the godliest men who ever lived, saying, in effect, "I was completely overwhelmed—I couldn't handle the situation I was in!"

All of us, whether we admit it or not, are control freaks (some of us more than others). I admit that I am "that guy"—the one who likes to be in control. Anytime I go somewhere with people, I have to drive. It's not that I think I'm the best driver in the world (although I'm pretty darn close); it's just that if I'm not driving,

I hate feeling out of control. On more than one occasion I've tried to put on the brakes in the passenger's side of the vehicle.

Because of this tendency to think I'm in charge, the Lord allows situations into my life to show me how out of control I am and to remind me that He really does have everything in His hands. As I heard a preacher say one time, "God is not an ambulance driver trying His best to get to every mess on the planet and clean it up!" He is Lord, and He holds everything in His capable hands.

Let's revisit the story of David and Goliath in 1 Samuel 17:4-7:

> Goliath, a Philistine champion from Gath, came out of the Philistine ranks to face the forces of Israel. He was over nine feet tall! He wore a bronze helmet, and his bronze coat of mail weighed 125 pounds. He also wore bronze leg armor, and he carried a bronze javelin on his shoulder. The shaft of his spear was as heavy and thick as a weaver's beam, tipped with an iron spearhead that weighed 15 pounds. His armor bearer walked ahead of him carrying a shield.

Goliath was huge—the largest enemy the Israelites had ever seen. In their minds they were already defeated and were simply delaying the inevitable. Eventually they would surrender and live under their enemies' control.

I'm sure there were some theological issues being discussed in the Israelites' camp as Goliath launched his taunts in their direction. There were probably guys asking, "If God loves us so much, how could He let this happen?" Or, "Someone once told me that God would never put more on me than I could manage. But this giant is way beyond us."

David's brothers thought Goliath was more than they could handle.

Saul thought Goliath was more than he could handle.

And David thought Goliath was more than he could handle.

Yep, you read that last sentence right. David knew he couldn't defeat Goliath on his own. He was well aware that the giant was highly trained and physically superior to him. He knew that according to logic, it would be a suicide mission to attempt to take this guy down. That's why David's statement in 1 Samuel 17:45 is so important:

> David replied to the Philistine, "You come to me with sword, spear, and javelin, but I come to you in the name of the LORD of Heaven's Armies—the God of the armies of Israel, whom you have defied."

David boasted not in his own strength but rather in the Lord's. He knew he didn't have what it took to handle the giant, but he knew God did. That was the difference between his unleashed life and the lives of the rest of the soldiers that cowered behind him. While they were trying to figure out how to handle this larger-than-life problem, David simply acknowledged that the Lord was in control. The rest is history.

At some point in our lives we will all face problems that are beyond us—challenges that are too big for us to handle on our own. There are three main truths we need to understand to help us get past those struggles with our faith intact.

TRUTH #1: Life is hard.

I'm not trying to depress anyone here, but I can't take some pie-in-the-sky approach and deny that we live in a fallen world where bad things happen.

In the book of 2 Chronicles, we are introduced to a king named

Jehoshaphat. As the king of Judah, he made some good decisions and some bad ones (just like all of us). In this passage we see him facing a particularly daunting situation:

> The armies of the Moabites, Ammonites, and some of the Meunites declared war on Jehoshaphat. Messengers came and told Jehoshaphat, "A vast army from Edom is marching against you from beyond the Dead Sea. They are already at Hazazon-tamar." (This was another name for En-gedi.)
>
> Jehoshaphat was terrified by this news and begged the LORD for guidance. He also ordered everyone in Judah to begin fasting. So people from all the towns of Judah came to Jerusalem to seek the LORD's help.
>
> 2 CHRONICLES 20:1-4

It's hard for me to wrap my mind around what a big deal this was because I happen to live in the United States of America. Our country hasn't been on the receiving end of many attacks in our history, and the thought that another country might invade our nation and completely take over has never really kept me awake at night.

However, for King Jehoshaphat and his people, this was a real threat. And the potentially tragic news that the enemy was on the attack came out of nowhere.

We've all been there, haven't we?

Just the other week I was in a hurry and was frantically running around my house trying to get out the door. I'd been in my basement lifting weights, and I had to take a shower because I pretty much smelled like death warmed over.

I'd forgotten that my wife had taken a shower the night before and that when she does, the floor of the tub is always a bit slippery the next day. I turned on the water so it could get hot (and so the soap on the floor could get extra slick). Then I literally jumped in the shower, hoping to get cleaned up as quickly as possible.

The next several seconds are still a blur.

I remember my feet hitting the soap-covered floor and then flying out from under me. I began to understand how much trouble I was in when I saw my feet go straight up in the air and realized that my head was on a collision course with an unforgiving surface.

I heard a loud crack, and then everything went fuzzy. The next thing I remember is lying there thinking, *Wow, I didn't see that coming.* (I am convinced that if the angels have YouTube in heaven, they've played "Naked Preacher Looks like an Idiot in the Shower" over and over again!)

Isn't that the way life happens? We're going along and everything is just fine—our health is good, there's enough to cover the bills, the job is going well—and then *bam*! something happens that takes us entirely by surprise. Something that leaves us completely overwhelmed.

If all along we've believed that God will never put more on us than we can handle, at this point we're bound to feel defeated and frustrated. If we can't handle what we're facing, then we assume something must be wrong with us. We must not have enough faith. We must not be living a godly enough life.

But I'm here to tell you that's simply not true. God often allows the "more" that happens to teach us to depend on His strength.

King Jehoshaphat was completely overwhelmed—he knew this situation was more than he could handle. We see his cry to God in 2 Chronicles 20:12:

> O our God, won't you stop them? We are powerless against this mighty army that is about to attack us. We do not know what to do, but we are looking to you for help.

In my mind, that might be one of the most humbling and powerful verses in the Bible. This king—the most powerful man in all the land, the guy who's supposed to have all the answers—tells God, "We are powerless against this mighty army." In other words, "God, this is way more than we can handle."

I'm sure we've all been there. Maybe for you the devastating news came in the form of a diagnosis, a termination, a dreaded announcement, a middle-of-the-night phone call. At one time or another, all of us have received that kick in the gut that leaves us overwhelmed, knowing there's no way we can get through this.

And it's usually at that point when some well-meaning-but-deceived Christian comes along and says, "Don't worry, God will never give you more than you can handle."

Wrong!

One of the most dangerous ideas we can buy into is that as long as we do everything "right"—as long as we check off the items on the list of good things God wants us to do—nothing bad will ever happen to us.

Scripture clearly teaches otherwise.

Joseph ran from temptation and consequently wound up in jail (see Genesis 39).

Shadrach, Meshach, and Abednego refused to bow before an idol, and as a result they were thrown into the furnace (see Daniel 3).

Job was doing absolutely nothing wrong; in fact, he was called "blameless" and "upright" by God Himself (Job 1:1, NIV). And yet all you-know-what broke loose in his life.

Paul and Silas were told to go to a certain region and preach the gospel, and before the chapter is over, we find them beaten and thrown into prison (see Acts 16).

Jesus never sinned, yet He was crucified.

Bad things happen to us not because of bad things we've done but because we live in a fallen world. Every time we face something we can't control, it's a reminder of how desperate we are for God, just as Jehoshaphat was.

TRUTH #2: God is still God.

One of the things that bothers me about life is that I'm often walking into situations where I don't know the outcome.

I love watching movies I've already seen because I know how they are going to end. I will also confess to skipping ahead and reading the last few pages of a book, because it kills me not to know how things are going to turn out.

Yet in life we can't fast-forward or find out the ending in advance. We have to walk with God step-by-step, trusting His power for each situation we face.

Several years ago I was in a developing country with a team from my church. We traveled all over the region to find the best place to serve the people in that part of the country.

One of our transportation arrangements for this trip was to take an airliner operated by the country we were in. I wasn't nervous . . . until we were getting ready to board the plane and I saw the aircraft. There was a dotted line drawn on the outside with these words written above the marking: "In case of emergency, cut here"!

When we sat down, a person from that country was sitting next to me. I immediately inquired about the airline. "Yes," he said. "This is our country's airline, and the planes we use are decommissioned aircrafts from Canada and the United States from the 1960s and 1970s."

The plane hadn't taken off yet, and already I needed that special paper bag from the seat pocket in front of me.

If that weren't enough, when the flight attendant was going

through the "safety features," about half of the oxygen masks dropped from the ceiling.

I wanted out of there! I was sure my life was over. I remember thinking as the plane took off, *I am so not in control!*

There are some moments we recognize it more than others, but we are *never* in control of our lives. We are, however, in control of the attitude we have as we face life.

Jehoshaphat found out that the enemy—one of the most powerful forces his nation had ever encountered—was coming against him. He acknowledged that the problem was too big for him and that he needed God's intervention. Then we see God's response to the situation:

> As all the men of Judah stood before the LORD with their little ones, wives, and children, the Spirit of the LORD came upon one of the men standing there. His name was Jahaziel son of Zechariah, son of Benaiah, son of Jeiel, son of Mattaniah, a Levite who was a descendant of Asaph.
>
> He said, "Listen, all you people of Judah and Jerusalem! Listen, King Jehoshaphat! This is what the LORD says: Do not be afraid! Don't be discouraged by this mighty army, for the battle is not yours, but God's. Tomorrow, march out against them. You will find them coming up through the ascent of Ziz at the end of the valley that opens into the wilderness of Jeruel. But you will not even need to fight. Take your positions; then stand still and watch the LORD's victory. He is with you, O people of Judah and Jerusalem. Do not be afraid or discouraged. Go out against them tomorrow, for the LORD is with you!"
>
> 2 CHRONICLES 20:13-17

In other words, God said, "I'm still in charge!"

After Jehoshaphat acknowledged that this enemy was more than he could handle, God clearly spoke to him. He said, in essence, "I've got this!" Just like Judah's king, we need to realize that God is God and that He isn't surprised by anything we're going through. He allowed the Israelites to become immersed in a situation that was completely overwhelming and beyond their control—not so they would "believe in themselves" more but rather so they would believe in Him and His power.

The key to King Jehoshaphat's success was not in seizing his own control and assuming responsibility over everything that was happening. Instead, he basically said to God, "I have no idea what's going on. I don't understand this. This is way more than I can handle. But I trust you!"

When we can't see or understand the Lord's will, we need to trust His Word.

If you find yourself overwhelmed by a situation that is seemingly too big for God to handle, take in a verse like 1 Peter 5:10:

> In his kindness God called you to share in his eternal glory by means of Christ Jesus. So after you have suffered a little while, he will restore, support, and strengthen you, and he will place you on a firm foundation.

In other words, God is God, and He's going to handle this.

Or if you're wondering if God is gone and if there's any hope for you, take a look at the truth found in Philippians 1:6:

> I am certain that God, who began the good work within you, will continue his work until it is finally finished on the day when Christ Jesus returns.

In other words, if God has led you to it, then He will lead you through it!

It isn't about who we are and what we can do but rather about who *God* is and what *He* can do.

Don't be afraid to admit there are things you can't handle—even if you're worried about those "plank-eyed" saints who are waiting to pounce all over you with judgmental attitudes. The truth is, God can and will put more on us than we can handle. But He does so to remind us that it isn't about who we are and what we can do but rather about who *He* is and what *He* can do.

TRUTH #3: You don't have to give up.

Being a parent has been one of the most joyous and most frustrating experiences of my life. Possibly one of the greatest challenges of parenting has been watching my little girl give up on something I know she is capable of. It breaks my heart at times because I can see how close she is to a breakthrough. But in her mind the circumstances seem overwhelming, so she throws in the towel. However, as her father, I can see what she can't see, and I desperately want her to persevere to the victory that's waiting just around the corner.

We won't give up on the God who has never given up on us.

I believe God longs for the same thing for His children. He wants us to acknowledge that we're in a situation that we cannot handle. That we're overwhelmed. That we have questions. That we don't understand. But that even in the face of daunting situations, we won't give up on the God who has never given up on us.

Take a look with me at the next part of Jehoshaphat's story:

King Jehoshaphat bowed low with his face to the ground. And all the people of Judah and Jerusalem did the same, worshiping the LORD. Then the Levites from the clans of Kohath and Korah stood to praise the LORD, the God of Israel, with a very loud shout.

Early the next morning the army of Judah went out into the wilderness of Tekoa. On the way Jehoshaphat stopped and said, "Listen to me, all you people of Judah and Jerusalem! Believe in the LORD your God, and you will be able to stand firm. Believe in his prophets, and you will succeed."

After consulting the people, the king appointed singers to walk ahead of the army, singing to the LORD and praising him for his holy splendor. This is what they sang:

"Give thanks to the LORD;
his faithful love endures forever!"

At the very moment they began to sing and give praise, the LORD caused the armies of Ammon, Moab, and Mount Seir to start fighting among themselves. The armies of Moab and Ammon turned against their allies from Mount Seir and killed every one of them. After they had destroyed the army of Seir, they began attacking each other. So when the army of Judah arrived at the lookout point in the wilderness, all they saw were dead bodies lying on the ground as far as they could see. Not a single one of the enemy had escaped.

King Jehoshaphat and his men went out to gather the plunder. They found vast amounts of equipment, clothing, and other valuables—more than they could

> carry. There was so much plunder that it took them three days just to collect it all! On the fourth day they gathered in the Valley of Blessing, which got its name that day because the people praised and thanked the LORD there. It is still called the Valley of Blessing today.
>
> Then all the men returned to Jerusalem, with Jehoshaphat leading them, overjoyed that the LORD had given them victory over their enemies. They marched into Jerusalem to the music of harps, lyres, and trumpets, and they proceeded to the Temple of the LORD.
>
> When all the surrounding kingdoms heard that the LORD himself had fought against the enemies of Israel, the fear of God came over them. So Jehoshaphat's kingdom was at peace, for his God had given him rest on every side.
>
> 2 CHRONICLES 20:18-30

Talk about an ending! God completely handled the situation and brought victory out of something that seemed certain to end in disaster.

No doubt it was painful for Jehoshaphat to admit he had no idea what to do. No doubt it was humbling for him to acknowledge that he was overwhelmed, at his wit's end, in over his head.

But fortunately for Jehoshaphat, he didn't try to fake it and tell everyone he was fine. He took off the bumper sticker on his camel that said God would never put more on him than he could handle. Instead, he made the decision to focus on the one he knew was in control—the one who would ultimately bring good out of the situation.

Through Jehoshaphat's story, we see that only God is able to take our pain and use it for progress.

Maybe at this point you're looking at your particular situation and asking, "How in the world can God bring good out of *this*?"

Honestly, I don't know. However, I do see in Scripture that God took a blood-stained cross and turned it into an empty tomb. And I have to believe that if He could do that, then He can use anything that we call pain for our progress.

Wherever you find yourself right now—if you're overwhelmed, confused, or maybe even considering throwing in the towel—I'm here to tell you, "Don't do it!"

Only God is able to take our pain and use it for progress.

I'm sure Jehoshaphat thought, *What's the point?* when he heard the news about the invading army.

I'd be willing to bet David's heartbeat sped up as he started walking toward the giant.

And even Jesus, on the night before His death, asked the Father to take the cup from Him if possible.

All of us face situations that tempt us to lose heart.

But we don't have to give up!

What if Jehoshaphat had given up as soon as the bad news came?

What if David had given up when he realized what he'd gotten himself into?

What if Jesus had given up as soon as the first stroke of the whip hit His back?

Anyone who has ever accomplished anything great in life has had to endure a significant amount of pain in order to get to where God wants them to be. The reason we feel overwhelmed, defeated, and frustrated is that we're only at the beginning of the story. God is bigger than our greatest fears; He's more powerful than our greatest enemies, and He can outlast our greatest frustrations. And although we don't know the end of our stories, He does.

So if you're tempted to give up, hang in there. Your Father sees you, and He is helping you. Hold on to this reminder from the apostle Paul:

> I can do everything through Christ, who gives me strength.
> PHILIPPIANS 4:13

Don't ever give up on the God who's never given up on you!

A new perspective on suffering

My friend Zac taught me more about walking with Jesus than any book I've read on the subject.

Several years ago Zac was diagnosed with cancer, which felt like an especially difficult blow since he was in his early 30s and had a wife and three children. I watched him and his family wrestle with this and beg God to heal him of his cancer.

In the midst of his illness, Zac did a video for our church, and at the end of it, he said something that since then has grown popular among the people at NewSpring Church. "If God chooses to heal me of this cancer," he said, "then God is God and God is good. And if He chooses not to heal me, then God is *still* God and God is *still* good. To God be the glory."

God is bigger than our greatest fears; He's more powerful than our greatest enemies, and He can outlast our greatest frustrations.

On May 16, 2010, Zac was healed of his cancer. But it wasn't in the way we all hoped. The Lord took him home, and it was a deeply emotional time for his family, his friends, and our church.

Less than a year later, his wife did her own video for our church and shared what the Lord had taught her through that season. The most powerful moment was at the end, when she said that she really believed, in spite of everything, "God is still God and God is still good. To God be the glory."

There's no way around it: life is hard. But no matter what circumstances we face, they don't change who God is. He is still God. When we truly believe that, it will transform our entire outlook on life, and we won't feel like there's no other option besides giving up.

I no longer preach sermons about how God will never give us more than we can handle, because I know firsthand that He does. But He also gives us what we need to endure whatever comes our way.

What in your life right now feels beyond your ability to manage? I encourage you not to feel like it's up to you to deal with this in your strength but to surrender that heavy load to the Lord.

> Give your burdens to the Lord,
> and he will take care of you.
>
> PSALM 55:22

Living an unleashed life doesn't mean that we never face trials; it just means that we press on with God's strength through those difficulties.

Still, you may not see me in a Speedo anytime soon.

CHAPTER 8

TAKE YOUR NEXT STEP

No matter what I tried, I could not sleep.

It was cold-and-flu season, and I had one of the most nagging coughs in the history of the modern world. Every minute or so it felt like something was lodged in my throat, causing me to cough for about a second. Then it was over.

A cough like that is easy enough to deal with during the day; however, it is one of the most annoying experiences when you're trying to go to sleep.

So every time I was about to doze off, I would wake up coughing. The longer this went on, the angrier I became, until finally I decided there was only one thing to do.

It was time to break out the Nyquil—a drug that absolutely knocks you out. I have a friend who calls it "the nighttime sniffling, sneezing, coughing, stuffy head, fever, why-did-I-wake-up-naked-in-the-bathtub medicine"!

I knew that all I needed was some Nyquil and my problems would be gone.

I got up and searched the apartment Lucretia and I were living in for the wonder drug that was going to put me in a coma . . . but none could be found. What was this? We had no Nyquil?

I'm sure you're thinking, *No problem—why didn't you just go and buy some?* Which is a logical thought, but by this time it was midnight, and believe it or not, there are hardly any stores open in Anderson, South Carolina, at midnight.

I knew I might not have any luck finding a store open that time of night, but I was desperate. So I drove around until I found a grocery store that was open twenty-four hours.

When I walked in, I noticed a lady by herself with a cart full of groceries. She was standing in front of a cash register, and there wasn't an employee anywhere in sight. I figured the person who was ringing up her order must have gone to do a price check or something, so I continued on to the medicine aisle, selected the cherry-flavored magic, and proceeded to the cash register to pay.

When I arrived, the lady was still standing there just looking around, so I stood behind her for a minute or two.

You may find this incredibly hard to believe, but I am not the most patient man on the planet. So after we'd stood there for two or three minutes, I asked her, "Have you seen an employee around here?"

"Nope," she answered.

"Wow!" I stared at her. "How long have you been standing here?"

"About fifteen minutes."

I couldn't believe it! Here was a woman who had done her grocery shopping at night (her cart was full) and had stood around just waiting for someone to help her when it was obvious that if anyone was in the store, that person was completely oblivious to her existence.

I decided to take the initiative to find someone (because I had to have my Nyquil!). I walked behind the cash register and found the intercom system, picked up the handset, and said over the loudspeaker, "Hello, store employees. I would love to inform you that there are customers at the front of the store who desire to make a purchase. We would deeply appreciate it if you would cease whatever activity you may be involved in and proceed to the front of the store, where you can total our orders for us so we can make our purchases and then leave."

After my little announcement I lined up behind the woman again, fully anticipating that someone would come along any second to assist us.

Nothing happened!

After another minute or two, I had this awful thought: *Oh no! Maybe the store was robbed before I arrived, and the employee who was working here is tied up somewhere and needs help.* I walked back to the intercom system and said, "This is the customer at the front of the store once again. It just occurred to me that you may have been robbed and are tied up somewhere in the store. If you will make some noise, I'll come and untie you. Then you can ring up this lady in front of me and sell me some Nyquil, and after that you can call the cops."

The lady, who until this point had just been standing there watching me, finally looked at me and said, "I can't believe you're doing this!" I wanted to reply, "I can't believe you're standing around in a grocery store just waiting for someone to help you when it's obvious no one is going to!" But I didn't.

In a matter of seconds, an employee ran around the corner, breathing hard and asking if we needed help. The lady told him that she thought I needed a lot of help and that it would make her happy if he would allow me to make my purchase first so I could get out of there.

I finally made it out of the store and back home, took my Nyquil, and dozed off into la-la land. However, all throughout the next day, I couldn't get the lady at the store out of my mind. She had stood there passively for twenty minutes when it was obvious someone needed to take action if any progress was going to be made.

It's sad, but many of us Christians act the same way. We stand around "waiting on God"—wanting great things to happen, yet refusing to take the initiative to actually do what the Lord wants us to do.

One of the things I often tell the church I serve is that Christianity is as simple as following Jesus one step at a time. As we do so, He will make us into who we need to be.

I love what Jesus told some of His first followers:

> As Jesus was walking beside the Sea of Galilee, he saw two brothers, Simon called Peter and his brother Andrew. They were casting a net into the lake, for they were fishermen. "Come, follow me," Jesus said, "and I will make you fishers of men."
>
> MATTHEW 4:18-19 (NIV, 1984)

Don't miss this: Jesus tells them that if they will follow Him, He will *make them* into who they need to be.

I think too many times, as followers of Christ, we get obsessed with issues that don't matter, or we stress over situations that exist only in our minds instead of focus on what's most important: simply following Him.

Christianity isn't just about praying a prayer that gets us out of hell. This life Jesus called us to live requires action after we've made the initial commitment to lay down our fishing nets and follow Him. We need to *surrender* fully to Jesus Christ and then *submit* to Him, step-by-step, for the rest of our lives. Christianity is not so much about what we've done but rather about who we are becoming.

If we want to continually experience the unleashing grace of God, then we have to always be willing to take the next step. We need to get past the "arrival mentality"—that somehow we've hit the high point of our spiritual maturity. We need to fight the desire to be satisfied with where we are in our walk with the Lord.

Christianity is not so much about what we've done but rather about who we are becoming.

The more I read the Bible, the more convinced I am that Jesus is always asking us to take the next step.

One thing that has always bothered me about "church folks" is that some people who have been Christians for decades have never changed—they are still just the same as they were twenty years ago. The longer some of us are involved in church and in Christianity, the more we seem to believe that we somehow have it all together.

Yet the reality, according to Scripture, is that we can't follow Jesus and stay the same. As we follow Him step-by-step, He makes us into who we need to be and shows us what we need to do.

I believe that every single one of us has a "next step" we need to take in our walk with Christ.

Let me give you an example from Scripture of someone who thought he was right on track, when nothing could have been further from the truth.

The apostle Paul was a godly man—not many people would doubt that statement. God used him to write most of the New Testament; he had most likely memorized the entire Old Testament, and on one occasion he prayed for someone who was dead and that person came back to life.

I'm pretty confident that none of the rest of us have pulled off all three of those things. It isn't a stretch to say that Paul was godlier than any of us.

With that in mind, let's take in what he wrote about himself:

> I want to know Christ and experience the mighty power that raised him from the dead. I want to suffer with him, sharing in his death, so that one way or another I will experience the resurrection from the dead!
>
> I don't mean to say that I have already achieved these things or that I have already reached perfection. But I press on to possess that perfection for which Christ Jesus first possessed me. No, dear brothers and sisters, I have not achieved it, but I focus on this one thing: Forgetting the past and looking forward to what lies ahead, I press on to reach the end of the race and receive the heavenly prize for which God, through Christ Jesus, is calling us.
>
> PHILIPPIANS 3:10-14

This is *Paul* here! And he's basically saying, "I haven't arrived. I still have a ways to go, and I'm going to do whatever it takes to make sure I take my next step."

Just because someone has attended church for thirty years, that doesn't mean that person is faithful. There is a big difference between attending church and following God.

David was a man who understood this concept. In fact, this is what the Bible says about him (from the lips of Paul himself):

> After removing Saul, [God] made David their king. He testified concerning him: "I have found David son of Jesse a man after my own heart; he will do everything I want him to do."
>
> ACTS 13:22, NIV

I don't know about you, but I want that! I don't just want to show up for church every week—I want to live a life where I do everything God wants me to do. However, this won't happen if I'm not willing to follow Him step-by-step.

So far in the story of David and Goliath we've seen a willingness in David to do what the Lord put in front of him and to follow what God wanted, one step at a time.

Remember, David didn't start out as a king or a big shot. He was just tending sheep, and then his father asked him to take his brothers some food. Once he got to the Israelite camp, he had a pretty difficult encounter with his brother Eliab. But ultimately he informed King Saul that he was willing to go into the valley to fight Goliath.

Don't miss this—David wasn't lucky! He wasn't some sort of overnight success. He was simply an ordinary person who believed in an extraordinary God and was willing to follow Him one little decision at a time.

But it doesn't stop there! Anyone can say they want to do this. Just about everyone I meet in the church world tells me that they want to do God's will, that they want to follow Him and do whatever He wants. Unfortunately, though, when it comes to taking action, too many of us are more like the lady in the grocery store—waiting for something to happen when it's obvious we need to take action.

Let's go back and look at 1 Samuel 17:32-37 again:

> "Don't worry about this Philistine," David told Saul. "I'll go fight him!"
>
> "Don't be ridiculous!" Saul replied. "There's no way you can fight this Philistine and possibly win! You're only a boy, and he's been a man of war since his youth."
>
> But David persisted. "I have been taking care of my father's sheep and goats," he said. "When a lion or a bear

> comes to steal a lamb from the flock, I go after it with a club and rescue the lamb from its mouth. If the animal turns on me, I catch it by the jaw and club it to death. I have done this to both lions and bears, and I'll do it to this pagan Philistine, too, for he has defied the armies of the living God! The Lord who rescued me from the claws of the lion and the bear will rescue me from this Philistine!"
>
> Saul finally consented. "All right, go ahead," he said. "And may the Lord be with you!"

Saul's immediate reaction was, "You can't do this!" (By the way, the first people to tell you not to do what God is clearly leading you to do are usually the ones who aren't being obedient themselves.)

David, on the other hand, essentially said, "I will take this next step."

David referred to God's faithfulness and assured Saul that with God's help, he could do this. Finally Saul said, "Go ahead. And may the Lord be with you."

This was where the rubber met the road, where the fertilizer hit the fan. It was time to either put up or shut up. David had a choice: he could back down, he could stand there, or he could embrace the "giant" opportunity God had placed in front of him.

At this point there was a lot David didn't know. I'm quite sure he was unaware of the war tactics the Philistines used. I'm positive he had little training in how to fight giants. I doubt very seriously he had any sort of degree in warfare.

But what he did have was a big God and the courage to put his faith in that big God. So what did he do?

> He picked up five smooth stones from a stream and put them into his shepherd's bag. Then, armed only with his

> shepherd's staff and sling, he started across the valley to fight the Philistine.
>
> 1 SAMUEL 17:40

David took his next step.

I'd like to ask you to hear me out on a theory. Bible experts take different sides on this point, but I believe it's worth mentioning.

We read in this verse that David picked up five smooth stones. Have you ever wondered why the writer of this story included that fact?

If we flip ahead to 2 Samuel, we see some additional details about this story:

> These four Philistines were descendants of the giants of Gath, but David and his warriors killed them.
>
> 2 SAMUEL 21:22

The writer of 2 Samuel talks about how four giants fell in battle, and some scholars believe they were actually the sons of Goliath. So the reason David picked up five stones may not have been because he was afraid he'd miss Goliath the first time but because he intended to take care of Goliath *and* his sons. His attitude was, *I'm going to complete what I began. I'm going to do whatever it takes*. Maybe that's why he's still known as a man after God's own heart.

David took the step to pick up the rocks, put them in his pouch, and approach Goliath.

So what are the rocks in *your* life that you need to pick up? In other words, what's your next step?

Maybe it is finally surrendering your life to Jesus—asking Him to come into your life as your Lord. You know His story. You know you're separated from God. You know you need to experience His forgiveness. But you're scared—scared of the changes you'll have to make and of what people might say. Here's my challenge: take that next step anyway, and allow Jesus to shape you and make you into who you need to be. The payoff for following Christ far outweighs any fears you might have.

Or maybe the rock you need to pick up is forgiving someone.

Maybe you need to stop having sex with the person you're not married to.

Maybe you need to end an ungodly dating relationship.

Maybe you need to surrender your finances and your spending habits to the Lord.

Maybe you need to control your temper.

Maybe you need to curb your gossip habit.

Most of us know our next step, yet so often we refuse to go for it. I believe there are three main reasons we don't do what we know we should do.

REASON #1: "I'll pray about it."

Let me be clear: I believe in the power of prayer. I've personally seen God do things through prayer that have absolutely floored me. Paul describes prayer as an offensive weapon given to followers of Christ (see Ephesians 6), and it's also a way for us to connect to the heart of God, as we see in the brutally honest prayers that pour out of David in the psalms.

However, having been in the church world for more than two decades now, I have come to the conclusion that sometimes we use prayer as an excuse for inactivity. We are afraid to act, so we use the idea of "waiting on God" as a crutch. All too often we'd rather pray than obey! But if we're truly praying about something and seeking God's direction, I believe He'll show us what to do next.

One of the passages from Scripture that has always stood out to me is Jeremiah 37:1-3:

> Zedekiah son of Josiah succeeded Jehoiachin son of Jehoiakim as the king of Judah. He was appointed by King Nebuchadnezzar of Babylon. But neither King Zedekiah nor his attendants nor the people who were left in the land listened to what the LORD said through Jeremiah.
>
> Nevertheless, King Zedekiah sent Jehucal son of Shelemiah, and Zephaniah the priest, son of Maaseiah, to ask Jeremiah, "Please pray to the LORD our God for us."

Here is an ungodly king, surrounded by ungodly leaders, who had no intention of following God. Yet he wanted Jeremiah to pray about something for him! He figured, *I'm going to do what I want to do, and as long as I pray about it, I'm going to be okay.*

Zedekiah wanted prayer, but he didn't actually want to do what God said. He believed that "praying about it" was all he needed to do to get God's blessing.

I once had a difficult conversation with a guy from my church about this issue of praying instead of acting. Every time I preached on sharing Christ with others, he would ask me to pray for his dad to be saved. This went on for about a year or two. One day when he approached me after a service and started to ask me the same thing again, I knew it was time to say something.

"Bob," I said (his name wasn't Bob—I'm totally making that up), "have you ever told your dad about Jesus or asked him if he's a Christian?"

Bob looked at me as if I were smoking crack. "No way! I could never do that. It would be uncomfortable—and way too hard!"

I looked at him for a moment. "Bob, I'm not going to pray for your dad to receive Christ."

He about passed out. I'm sure he'd never had a pastor tell him that before. But I recognized that Bob was doing something so many of us do: he was using prayer as an excuse for inactivity. He was asking me to pray for his dad to be saved, but he was unwilling to actually talk to his dad about salvation.

"I won't pray for your dad," I continued. "But I will pray for *you*. I will pray for you to have the courage to go to your dad and have a conversation about Jesus. I will pray for you to have strength like never before so you can do this. And then I will pray that you will watch your father come to Christ, not through the prayers of your pastor, but rather through your obedience and your willingness to take the step He is obviously leading you to take."

Think about it this way: what if David had simply prayed that God would get rid of Goliath but he never took any action? This story probably wouldn't be in the Bible.

I dearly love my daughter, Charisse. Let's say I go home this afternoon and ask her to please pick up a piece of paper from the kitchen floor and put it into the trash can. If she does, we can move on. And if at any point she doesn't fully understand what I'm telling her to do, she can ask questions for clarification.

However, if she simply stands over the piece of paper for the rest of the day and asks me, "Do you really want me to take this piece of paper and put it in the trash can?" then I believe we have a problem. I'm the father, and I've spoken as clearly as possible. If she wants to have a conversation about my command rather than obey it, then something is not right.

The same thing can be said of our walk with God. Yes, there are times we need to pray through the specifics of a situation. However, there are some things God has already made clear, and we don't need to spend lots of time waiting for an answer about how to proceed. For example, we never have to pray about whether we should forgive. We never have to pray about whether we should remain sexually pure. We never have to pray about whether to have an affair. We never have to pray about whether we should share the truth and grace of Christ with our loved ones. And we never have to pray about whether to put Him first in our lives. We just need to take the steps He has clearly called us to take.

Don't waste your Father's time having a conversation about a command He has clearly communicated to you.

REASON #2: Disobedience

Has anyone ever given you the middle finger?

Maybe it was in school or in traffic or during a heated argument. Whatever the situation, I'm sure you didn't consider it to be a sign of affection.

Now let's take this a step further. If you're a parent, let's say you walk into your house and ask your child to clean his room and instead he simply looks at you and gives you the finger.

No good parent would tolerate that type of behavior. (My parents would have broken off my finger!)

You may not realize it, but this is what we do sometimes in our relationship with God. When God has clearly spoken to us about our next step and we tell Him no, we're essentially extending our middle finger toward heaven.

The following passage about the prophet Ezekiel has always captivated my attention as an example of what happens when people show blatant disregard for God's commands:

> Some of the leaders of Israel visited me [Ezekiel], and while they were sitting with me, this message came to me from the Lord: "Son of man, these leaders have set

> up idols in their hearts. They have embraced things that will make them fall into sin. Why should I listen to their requests? Tell them, 'This is what the Sovereign LORD says: The people of Israel have set up idols in their hearts and fallen into sin, and then they go to a prophet asking for a message. So I, the LORD, will give them the kind of answer their great idolatry deserves. I will do this to capture the minds and hearts of all my people who have turned from me to worship their detestable idols.'
>
> "Tell the people of Israel, 'This is what the Sovereign LORD says: Repent and turn away from your idols, and stop all your detestable sins.'"
>
> EZEKIEL 14:1-6

The quick recap here is that a group of people comes to Ezekiel hoping he'll ask God, "What's next for us? Help us out—give us some insight."

And God says back to them, "I'm going to deal with the sin in your life right now. And until we deal with that, you're stuck."

Why would God trust us with what's next if we aren't obedient with what He's showing us now? We're called to be His faithful followers, and faithfulness is determined by how we are obeying God right now, not by promising what we'll do if He gives us more insight or more blessings.

Why would God trust us with what's next if we aren't obedient with what He's showing us now?

It is impossible to experience spiritual maturity while hanging on to an area of disobedience.

Often when God is dealing with us in a certain area and we don't want to surrender it to Him, we try to immerse ourselves in some sort of Christian activity. We falsely believe that doing so will somehow appease God and He'll give us a pass about our pet sin.

However, just as a Diet Coke doesn't cancel out a double cheeseburger, more "obedience" in other areas of our lives doesn't cancel out blatant disobedience in one area.

Being stuck is *not* a good place to be. For one thing, God isn't going to change His mind about your situation—sin will always be sin.

If God is bringing up some area of disobedience in your life, be thankful. He does that not so He can beat you up about it but because He loves you and He wants anything that can hurt you out of your life.

Procrastination is assassination on the amazing future God has for you.

REASON #3: Procrastination

Procrastination is assassination on the amazing future God has for you.

When you know what God wants for your life, go for it! Don't hesitate. Don't put it off until you're older or wiser or have more resources.

David didn't procrastinate. He didn't sit around and form a discussion group; he simply saw God's next step for him, and he embraced the opportunity.

> Goliath walked out toward David with his shield bearer ahead of him, sneering in contempt at this ruddy-faced boy. "Am I a dog," he roared at David, "that you come at me with a stick?" And he cursed David by the names of his gods. "Come over here, and I'll give your flesh to the birds and wild animals!" Goliath yelled.
>
> David replied to the Philistine, "You come to me with

> sword, spear, and javelin, but I come to you in the name of the LORD of Heaven's Armies—the God of the armies of Israel, whom you have defied. Today the LORD will conquer you, and I will kill you and cut off your head. And then I will give the dead bodies of your men to the birds and wild animals, and the whole world will know that there is a God in Israel! And everyone assembled here will know that the LORD rescues his people, but not with sword and spear. This is the LORD's battle, and he will give you to us!"
>
> 1 SAMUEL 17:41-47

Goliath came after David with harsh words and tried to scare him out of what God told him to do. But it didn't slow David down one bit.

Whenever we attempt to do something significant for God, the enemy will attack us with intimidation and manipulation. If we want to follow Christ step-by-step, there will always be that voice in our heads saying, *Oh, you can do that later*. It's a battle all of us have to fight if we want to take a step forward for Christ.

I'll never forget a conversation I had with a friend in August 1999 over lunch at Red Lobster. He was mentoring me and helping me through one of the most confusing times I'd ever experienced. I knew God wanted me to do something—I knew He was leading me to take a step of faith—but I was unsure what it was.

After we talked for a while, my mentor looked at me and asked a question that changed the entire course of my life. "Perry," he said, "what would you be willing to attempt for God if you knew you could not fail?"

I didn't even blink. Without hesitation I said, "I would start a church!"

"And you are a coward if you don't!" he replied.

I was freaked out! I had never been a pastor. I had no money. I had no knowledge of how to start a church. Still, I made the decision right there in the restaurant booth that I was going to take that step because I firmly believed that's what God was calling me to do. It wasn't an easy decision—in fact, I'm not sure I slept for three or four nights. But I wasn't going to stall by endlessly praying about it. I wasn't going to give God the middle finger by disobeying Him. I simply surveyed the situation, reviewed all that God had done in my life up to that point, and knew this was what God had planned for me.

Now, something you need to understand about me is that I love doughnuts. *Love* them. But my favorite doughnuts in the world, hands down, are hot, glazed doughnuts from Krispy Kreme.

We don't have a Krispy Kreme in Anderson, South Carolina, so if I want their hot doughnuts, it has to be when I'm out of town.

I remember on one occasion my plane landed in Daytona Beach, Florida, and I was on my way to the hotel to get unpacked and settled in. (Since I'm a bit type A, this is always a priority for me when I arrive somewhere.) I was driving down the road with thoughts of what I was going to speak on that evening when, all of a sudden, everything changed.

We passed a Krispy Kreme, and the "Hot Now" sign was on.

Now if you've never had this life-altering experience, the "Hot Now" sign means that fresh, hot doughnuts have just been made and are available for consumption.

The "Hot Now" sign changed my course that day! No longer was I thinking about unpacking or speaking or traffic laws. I had to have a doughnut—several, actually!

But if I was going to seize the opportunity, I couldn't procrastinate. I couldn't unpack at my leisure and then drive back later in the afternoon or when my speaking event was finished and expect the sign to still be on. The moment was now, and I needed to make a decision to go for it.

Of course, what that doughnut shop has to offer pales in comparison to what God has in store for us. And He gives us clear indications—almost as obvious as the "Hot Now" sign—about what our next step is. The question isn't so much what we should do but whether we're going to do what He has already instructed us to do.

The conversation I had with my mentor in Red Lobster that summer day absolutely changed the trajectory of my life. I walked out of the restaurant with not only the knowledge of what God wanted me to do but also the willingness to make it happen. I wasn't going to put if off or just pray about it endlessly. The sign was clear, and I was ready to act.

Learning to trust

Taking the next step isn't easy. Which is why we have to learn to trust God.

Scripture frequently uses the metaphor of God as a perfect Father, and now that I'm a dad, that makes a lot of sense to me.

Ever since my daughter, Charisse, was a toddler, I've put her in high places and told her, "Jump to Daddy." At first she was hesitant, but after a lot of encouragement, she started embracing the challenge. Gradually she has started jumping off higher and higher places. It's no problem for her because I've always caught her in the past.

Now how jacked up would it be if I started dropping her? Or, even worse, if I pretended I was going to catch her and didn't? It breaks my heart to even think about that. I love my daughter, and I would never do something like that. Whenever I place her in a situation where she has to take a step of faith and trust me, I want her to be confident that she's jumping into the arms of a daddy who wants nothing but the best for her.

Why in the world would we think anything less of our heavenly Father?

You may be wrestling with your next step, and it may be one of the most challenging things God has ever called you to do. But I believe that if God has led you to this, then He won't leave you to face it alone. And it just may be that He has brought you to this place so you can learn to trust Him more.

David knew a thing or two about trusting God. Let's take a look at the next part of his story:

> As Goliath moved closer to attack, David quickly ran out to meet him. Reaching into his shepherd's bag and taking out a stone, he hurled it with his sling and hit the Philistine in the forehead. The stone sank in, and Goliath stumbled and fell face down on the ground.
>
> So David triumphed over the Philistine with only a sling and a stone, for he had no sword. Then David ran over and pulled Goliath's sword from its sheath. David used it to kill him and cut off his head.
>
> When the Philistines saw that their champion was dead, they turned and ran. Then the men of Israel and Judah gave a great shout of triumph and rushed after the Philistines, chasing them as far as Gath and the gates of Ekron. The bodies of the dead and wounded Philistines were strewn all along the road from Shaaraim, as far as Gath and Ekron. Then the Israelite army returned and plundered the deserted Philistine camp. (David took the Philistine's head to Jerusalem, but he stored the man's armor in his own tent.)
>
> 1 SAMUEL 17:48-54

David kept taking his next steps. The giant ran toward him; he ran toward the giant. He pulled out a stone, put it in his sling, and slung it. After it knocked Goliath to the ground, David pulled out the giant's sword and cut off his head, which is exactly what he said he would do.

Each time he faced the next decision, David simply took his next step. And in doing so, he went from bringing snacks to his brothers to defeating the most powerful enemy the Israelites had ever faced. Simply because he followed the Lord one step at a time.

Later in his life, David (who was something of a poet when he wasn't off fighting giants) wrote about trusting God in the face of danger:

> Even when I walk
> through the darkest valley,
> I will not be afraid,
> for you are close beside me.
> Your rod and your staff
> protect and comfort me.
>
> PSALM 23:4

Let's be honest—we've made Christianity way too difficult. Being a Christian isn't about obtaining a certain measure of theological knowledge; it isn't about reading a certain version of the Bible for a certain length of time every day; it isn't about putting cheesy bumper stickers on our cars or wearing certain types of clothes.

The reality is that we can't walk with Jesus and stay the same.

Being a Christian is about surrendering to Jesus and then submitting to Him on a daily basis, one step at a time, and knowing that as we do so, He's going to make us into who we need to be.

The reality is that we can't walk with Jesus and stay the same. He has called us to follow Him, which means He is going somewhere. Following Him isn't always the easiest thing, but it's always the right thing. And it's possible—not because of our own heroic efforts but because we're putting our trust in a powerful God who cares specifically about us.

So what is that next step you are wrestling with right now? Are you going to avoid action by saying you'll pray about it? Are you going to blatantly disobey what God is calling you to do? Are you going to put it off, promising you'll do it later?

The unleashed life can start right now . . . with just a single step!

CHAPTER 9

WE CAN'T DO LIFE ALONE

Sometimes life happens and situations hit that we're unprepared to face. It's during those times that we desperately need the help and community of other people. This truth became real to me one day when I was working out in the gym.

To say that I'm intense when I work out is sort of like saying the Pope is a bit Catholic. When I'm at the gym, I'm there for one purpose: to push myself as hard as I can. I like to rev up my heart rate as much as possible until my chest is really pounding.

One of the most effective ways I've found for pushing my workout to the limits is something called interval training.

Interval training, when done properly, will cause you to beg God for things like oxygen and/or the Rapture. For me, interval training looks something like this: I get on a treadmill and find a nice, comfortable pace to do a jog or a light run for about a minute. Then I crank up the machine to a pace that throws me into an all-out sprint for thirty seconds. Afterward I decrease my speed to a light run again for a minute, and then I sprint for another thirty seconds. I repeat this cycle for at least twenty minutes.

One day when I was at the gym doing this interval training, I was really feeling it, so I decided to push myself a little harder than usual. On my final interval, I maxed out the speed on the machine. After sprinting for thirty seconds, I hit the stop button, feeling certain my heart was on the verge of exploding. I promised God that if He would allow me to recover, I would never do anything like that again.

I somehow managed to walk to the water fountain and get a few sips of water. Then I climbed on the exercise bike directly behind the treadmill to cool down a little.

That's when I saw the cute little old lady get on the treadmill I'd just been on.

Before I go on, I need to explain something I would discover just a minute or so later: the treadmill I'd been on had a mechanical issue. You see, most treadmills automatically reset after someone hits the stop button, so when the next user starts the machine, it's supposed to move at a slow pace. Apparently, however, this treadmill wasn't working properly. So when the next person hit start, it resumed the pace set by the previous user.

The little old lady stepped onto the machine with a smile on her face, having no clue I'd exited the treadmill at maximum speed. She had no idea what was waiting for her the moment she hit that start button.

I saw her step on the treadmill, and then something on the television screen caught my attention. All of a sudden I heard the sound of a jet taking off and someone screaming, "Help!" at the top of her lungs. I glanced at the treadmill and saw this lady holding on to the arm rails with a look of terror on her face, her legs flying out behind her.

At that point she didn't need someone to pray for her. She

didn't need to read a book titled *Ten Ways to Escape the Treadmill of Death*. She didn't need advice or some sort of cute jewelry with a cross on it to remind her that Jesus is always with her.

She needed someone to come alongside her and unplug the treadmill!

I leaped off the bike, ran over, and ripped the plug out of the outlet. Then I helped her sit down against a wall. The woman's husband, who had been on the rowing machine at the back of the gym, ran over and thanked me for saving her life. I wasn't sure I'd exactly rescued her from the jaws of death, but I was starting to grasp that she could have been in some trouble if I hadn't been close enough to help her out.

As I walked out of the gym that day, I couldn't get that woman out of my mind. I'm sure she'd shown up at the gym that day expecting to walk on the treadmill at a nice, comfortable pace for about twenty minutes and then go home and maybe even bake an apple pie.

But life didn't turn out quite like she'd anticipated. She hit the start button, and before she knew it, she was in trouble—and quite unable to get herself out of the situation on her own. There's no way she could have rescued herself. She needed help!

And so do we all.

Like the lady on the treadmill, have you ever had a day when something hit you out of nowhere?

You find out your spouse has been seeing someone else.

Your boss informs you that the company is downsizing, and you're on your way out.

Your doctor calls and says the results of your recent exam have raised some concerns.

The police department calls and wants to talk with you about your teenager.

Someone close to you steps into eternity.

Whatever the specifics, life happens. We all have those "treadmill moments." And if we aren't careful, those situations can send us flying off course, derailing us from the purpose God has for us. We wind up feeling trapped and helpless and alone.

How do we survive those tough times? Is it possible to live an unleashed life even when everything around us is falling apart? It is possible—but to do so, we have to be willing to let other people into our lives. God never meant for us to do life alone.

One of the things I've always admired about David is that he never attempted to face life without the help of others. In fact, immediately after the Bible records his victory over Goliath, we read about a friendship that forms between David and King Saul's son Jonathan.

> After David had finished talking with Saul, he met Jonathan, the king's son. There was an immediate bond between them, for Jonathan loved David. From that day on Saul kept David with him and wouldn't let him return home. And Jonathan made a solemn pact with David, because he loved him as he loved himself. Jonathan sealed the pact by taking off his robe and giving it to David, together with his tunic, sword, bow, and belt.
>
> 1 SAMUEL 18:1-4

Jonathan came alongside David and did life with him through significant ups and downs. Jonathan celebrated with him in his victories and wept with him when he faced difficult times. When things between King Saul (Jonathan's father) and David took a turn for the worse, Jonathan defended David (see 1 Samuel 19:1-5). He even put his own life in danger to protect his friend (see 1 Samuel 20:24-42). David wouldn't have been able to make it on his own without his friend Jonathan.

When David was on the run from psycho King Saul, we see that David continued to surround himself with people who would support him:

> David left Gath and escaped to the cave of Adullam. Soon his brothers and all his other relatives joined him there. Then others began coming—men who were in trouble or in debt or who were just discontented—until David was the captain of about 400 men.
>
> 1 SAMUEL 22:1-2

David was being hunted down by a powerful leader who wanted to take his life. He could have given in to the temptation to isolate himself from other people, to throw a pity party where he was the guest of honor. He could have allowed his circumstances to push him to a place of loneliness and hidden in a cave all alone.

Yet when people began to gather around him, he didn't push them away or tell them he'd be fine. Instead, he received them into his life, and the Lord used those people to eventually bring David to a position of leadership in his country.

I've always been moved by the list of David's "mighty men," many of whom stayed by his side for his entire life. These loyal warriors accomplished some pretty remarkable feats under David's leadership: they slayed giants, overcame incredible odds in battle, and chased lions into pits (see 2 Samuel 23:8-39). They achieved far more as a group than David ever could have accomplished on his own. David knew he needed them if he was going to accomplish what God had called him to do.

We never become who God wants us to be or accomplish all He wants us to accomplish by ourselves. We all need the support of other believers to help us live out God's unleashing grace.

Do we really need one another?

Did you know that the phrase "one another" appears more than fifty times in the New Testament alone? So either God has a stuttering problem or He's trying to emphasize a point. We need one another in order to live the unleashed life.

God has given us two essentials to help us experience true community.

The first is the church.

I know, I know—the church has "issues." Many people have been hurt and mistreated by the church, and their stories are heartbreaking. The truth is, there isn't a single church on the planet that is perfect—all of them are full of imperfect people, and if we stay in one long enough, something negative or hurtful is bound to happen to us.

However, in spite of all the bad things that have happened in the church, God still considers it the bride of Christ. He loves the church, and His plan is to use it as His primary tool to impact the world. We need to be careful about consistently bad-mouthing the church; after all, if you were to tell me that you really like me but you think my bride is ugly, one of us is going to get hurt. It's the same with Christ. When we dis the church, we are dissing His bride—and that can't be good for our relationship with Him.

The second gift God gives us is the Christ-focused relationships we have within the church.

It's not enough to just attend a church service every week or so and then dart to the car and speed out of the parking lot as soon as the service is over. Sure, we might learn a thing or two about the Bible and even pray as we sprint out the door, but if that's the extent of it, we're missing out on one of the greatest resources a church can offer: the people in it. These people aren't perfect; they're humans just like you and me, and they have their share of ups and downs. But God has placed them in our lives so we can serve them when they're struggling and so they can help us in our own times of need.

I've never met anyone who told me, "Hey, Perry, I really want to go further and further away from God and backslide in my walk with Him. I hope to make a really bad decision followed by a series of more bad decisions that eventually lead to sorrow, pain, and regret." Even so, I've seen it happen many times. As human beings, our tendency is to drift away from Christ rather than to walk more closely with Him. If we're not intentional about seeking out the help of others, that's precisely what's going to happen.

One of the stories that has often caused me to scratch my head in disbelief is the one about the apostle Peter near the time of Jesus' arrest and crucifixion.

> Peter was sitting outside in the courtyard. A servant girl came over and said to him, "You were one of those with Jesus the Galilean."
>
> But Peter denied it in front of everyone. "I don't know what you're talking about," he said.
>
> Later, out by the gate, another servant girl noticed him and said to those standing around, "This man was with Jesus of Nazareth."
>
> Again Peter denied it, this time with an oath. "I don't even know the man," he said.
>
> A little later some of the other bystanders came over to Peter and said, "You must be one of them; we can tell by your Galilean accent."
>
> Peter swore, "A curse on me if I'm lying—I don't know the man!" And immediately the rooster crowed.
>
> Suddenly, Jesus' words flashed through Peter's mind:

> "Before the rooster crows, you will deny three times that you even know me." And he went away, weeping bitterly.
> MATTHEW 26:69-75

This was Jesus' right-hand man—you know, the one who, according to every joke about heaven, always meets people at the gate. This was the guy who actually walked on water while his friends stayed in the boat (see Matthew 14:22-33). This was the man who boldly proclaimed that Jesus was the Messiah (see Matthew 16:16). This was the one person who should have had his act together and boldly acknowledged Christ at every opportunity.

And yet he denied Jesus—not once, but three times. It seems that Peter's denial got easier each time, and by his third claim not to know Christ, he was actually calling down curses on himself.

How in the world does this happen? How does someone go from promising Jesus he'll never deny Him (see Matthew 26:31-35) to denying Him three times in the span of one night?

It's quite simple, actually: Peter isolated himself not only from Jesus but also from others who followed Jesus. In doing so, he found himself plunged into denial and regret.

If the apostle Peter needed people to keep him on track, it must be true for us as well.

Let's take a closer look at Peter's story to see what it can show us about the importance of having other people in our lives.

Peter's walk with Christ started out with an impressive beginning. Jesus called Peter to follow Him, and Peter did so immediately, leaving behind all that was familiar and walking away from his family fishing business (see Matthew 4:18-20). For the next three years Peter regularly had his mind blown as he began to understand who Jesus is.

As Peter followed Christ, he began to understand that Jesus

never asks anyone to follow Him halfheartedly. Jesus always wants all-out commitment.

Peter lived out the high calling we read about in Hebrews 10:23 (NIV):

> Let us hold unswervingly to the hope we profess, for he who promised is faithful.

That verse moves me to want to go all out in my walk with Christ. Like Peter when he first started following Christ, I want to jump in with both feet and hold on without swerving. As one of my favorite speakers says, "A 95 percent commitment to Christ is 5 percent too short."

All too often, though, we are tempted to swerve in our walks with Christ. We don't set out to intentionally sabotage our faith, of course. But by nature we are inclined toward the things that satisfy our flesh rather than toward the things that are pleasing to God. So, like Peter when he denied even knowing Jesus, we end up swerving from our true purpose.

Whenever I think about holding "unswervingly" to Christ, I can't help but recall the night the possum almost killed me and a car full of friends.

As an aside, I have to say that some of God's creatures make me scratch my head. I'm not quite sure why He made the mosquito or the spider. (I used to question His creation of cats until I came to the conclusion that He must have allowed Satan to create one thing . . . and that's where the cat came from!) However, one of the creatures that puzzles me most is the possum.

Unless you live in the southeastern part of the United States, you may not even know what a possum is. And even if you do live in an area where these creatures live, you've probably only seen them dead on the side of the road. They're often out late at night rummaging for food, and since they have terrible vision, they tend to walk right out in front of cars.

One night I was driving down the road with a carful of my friends when all of a sudden Mr. Possum decided to stroll directly in the path of my car.

I swerved!

As I jerked the car to the right, I felt us sliding sideways and heard the tires screaming. So I did what is commonly referred to as overcompensating—I immediately turned the car in the other direction. As a result, we started doing doughnuts in the middle of the road. Everyone in the car was screaming—and most likely in need of a change of underwear by the time it was all over. If there had been a car in the other lane, it would have been a disaster.

Believe me, I don't swerve for animals anymore. Since that time, numerous animals have met their Maker after running in front of my car. But I've seen the damage swerving can do. It almost cost me my life, and I simply refuse to do it anymore.

We need to be just as committed in our walk with Christ. Even though Jesus Christ saved us from the penalty of sin, we still have to deal with the presence of sin every day. When sin runs out in front of us, our immediate reaction is to swerve from the path God has put us on.

Our friends at college are going down a path we know is wrong, but we can't find the strength to do what is right. So we swerve.

Our boss asks us to do something that compromises our integrity. We know we shouldn't, but we desperately need a promotion. So we swerve.

We are dating someone we know we shouldn't be with, but all our friends are getting married, and we don't want to be left out. So we swerve.

We log on to the computer late one night. We know we shouldn't visit that website, but we just can't seem to stop ourselves. So we swerve.

All of us, no matter how close we're walking with Jesus, are tempted to veer off the path and do something we know we shouldn't do. It's not because we're bad people but rather because we live in a world that is working against anyone who has a desire to follow Jesus.

That's when we need guardrails.

The best guardrails I've found to keep me on the right path are godly relationships. God knows there are times I lack the strength to walk through difficult situations on my own, so He places people in my life who will be strong when I am weak. As a result, I've been able to face and overcome far more than I could have on my own.

Godly friends are the people in the car who can see the possum before we do. They keep us on course in spite of what the enemy throws our way.

If the apostle Peter had surrounded himself with his friends and fellow believers at his lowest moment, it's possible things might have turned out differently for him in that moment. But in his isolation and loneliness, he ended up denying Jesus.

It's easy to think, *That will never happen to me,* most likely because we've fallen victim to one of the four lies that make us think we don't need the support of others.

LIE #1: Salvation is enough to keep me strong.

I will never forget the day I trusted Christ to come into my life, forgive my sins, and take over as my Lord. It was May 27, 1990. Starting at that moment, I was on a high I'd never experienced before. I was passionate about reading my Bible and praying, and I was quite sure I'd never sin again in my entire life.

About two weeks later, a girl at work made me mad—really mad. The kind of mad that turns your face three shades of red and causes your blood pressure to max out. Before I knew it, in my anger, I'd dropped the "f bomb."

What? Where did that come from? I couldn't understand how something like this could happen! I hadn't cussed since I'd received Christ, and all of a sudden the word flew out of me like a bat out of hades. Was I still a Christian? Was I going to hell?

I freaked out because I'd believed the lie that once I became a Christian, I would never swerve—ever.

Then as I continued to read the Bible, I discovered that even people who follow Jesus aren't exempt from being screwed up, sinful, dysfunctional human beings. The idea that we'll never wrestle with sin once we're on the other side of the Cross is a myth. Even the apostle Paul had this struggle:

> The trouble is not with the law, for it is spiritual and good. The trouble is with me, for I am all too human, a slave to sin. I don't really understand myself, for I want to do what is right, but I don't do it. Instead, I do what I hate. But if I know that what I am doing is wrong, this shows that I agree that the law is good. So I am not the one doing wrong; it is sin living in me that does it.
>
> And I know that nothing good lives in me, that is, in my sinful nature. I want to do what is right, but I can't. I want to do what is good, but I don't. I don't want to do what is wrong, but I do it anyway. But if I do what I don't want to do, I am not really the one doing wrong; it is sin living in me that does it.
>
> I have discovered this principle of life—that when I want to do what is right, I inevitably do what is wrong.
>
> ROMANS 7:14-21

If Paul wrestled with sin and the temptation to swerve, then there's no question we will as well. The battle wasn't over once he was saved.

I thank God for my salvation. The more I understand how dead I was in my sin, the more overwhelmed I become that He has made me alive again. However, salvation is not the finish line but rather the starting block. Our lives will be full of victories and defeats, and we need to be prepared for the challenges that lie ahead of us once we decide to follow Christ.

Salvation is not the finish line but rather the starting block.

Let's take a look at Peter's decision to follow Jesus' call:

> One day as Jesus was walking along the shore of the Sea of Galilee, he saw two brothers—Simon, also called Peter, and Andrew—throwing a net into the water, for they fished for a living. Jesus called out to them, "Come, follow me, and I will show you how to fish for people!" And they left their nets at once and followed him.
>
> MATTHEW 4:18-20

Here we see that the apostle Peter had a genuine salvation experience. Jesus clearly called Peter to follow Him, and he responded by putting his fishing nets down to be with the Fisher of people. Peter met Christ that day and spent the next several years getting an inside glimpse into who He was. And yet when it came down to the critical moment, Peter denied Him.

The takeaway for us is that salvation is not enough to sustain our devotion to Christ. We can't expect to stay strong without the support of community.

LIE #2: Emotion will sustain my devotion.

If our faithfulness to Christ is built on one emotional experience after the other, then we're headed for a spiritual train wreck. Let me explain by telling you a story.

You probably don't remember where you were on October 21, 2006, but I remember it quite well.

I love college football, and my favorite team is the Clemson Tigers. I've been a Clemson fan ever since I can remember, and there's nothing quite like being in Death Valley (the nickname of their stadium) and watching them dominate their opponent.

On that October day in 2006, the Tigers were playing one of their rivals, Georgia Tech. Both teams were nationally ranked, it was a night game, and ESPN's *GameDay* was there. Needless to say, the atmosphere was electric.

Without going into too much detail, I'll just say that Clemson absolutely whipped Georgia Tech's rear end. The final score was 31–7, and I can honestly say I've never heard the stadium as loud as it was that evening. People were going crazy, proclaiming their love for Clemson and declaring that they were the greatest football team to have ever walked the earth. I think I even witnessed a few people throwing their babies onto the field.

Emotions were at an all-time high. Clemson was on a roll. No one and nothing could stop this team.

Less than a week later, on October 26, Clemson played a Thursday night game at Virginia Tech. Honestly, it is too painful for me to write about. The game was nationally televised on ESPN, which made the humiliation all the more public. We didn't just lose; we got pounded.

But the most surprising part was the fans' attitude, which did a 180 in a few short days. After the Georgia Tech game, people were insisting that the head coach be nominated as the fourth member of the Trinity, and after the Virginia Tech game, they were demanding that he be cast into the eternal lake of fire.

I learned an important lesson that night: emotion does *not* sustain devotion. Not in football, and not in Christianity either.

Let's take a look at another emotionally charged event in Peter's life:

> Peter called to [Jesus], "Lord, if it's really you, tell me to come to you, walking on the water."
>
> "Yes, come," Jesus said.
>
> So Peter went over the side of the boat and walked on the water toward Jesus. But when he saw the strong wind and the waves, he was terrified and began to sink. "Save me, Lord!" he shouted.
>
> Jesus immediately reached out and grabbed him. "You have so little faith," Jesus said. "Why did you doubt me?"
>
> MATTHEW 14:28-31

Peter walked on water!

Peter often gets criticized for his lack of faith, but let's not forget there were eleven other disciples who never left the boat.

Later in Peter's walk with Jesus, he had the ultimate mountain-top experience:

> Jesus took Peter and the two brothers, James and John, and led them up a high mountain to be alone. As the men watched, Jesus' appearance was transformed so that his face shone like the sun, and his clothes became as white as light. Suddenly, Moses and Elijah appeared and began talking with Jesus.
>
> Peter exclaimed, "Lord, it's wonderful for us to be here! If you want, I'll make three shelters as

> memorials—one for you, one for Moses, and one for Elijah."
>
> But even as he spoke, a bright cloud overshadowed them, and a voice from the cloud said, "This is my dearly loved Son, who brings me great joy. Listen to him." The disciples were terrified and fell face down on the ground.
>
> Then Jesus came over and touched them. "Get up," he said. "Don't be afraid." And when they looked up, Moses and Elijah were gone, and they saw only Jesus.
>
> MATTHEW 17:1-8

Talk about an emotional experience. Within a few seconds Peter saw two famous prophets show up who were supposedly dead, he watched Jesus' face light up brighter than the Griswold house in *Christmas Vacation*, and he heard the audible voice of God. I'm guessing none of us have come close to something like that. But Peter was there as a firsthand witness.

And yet this guy who walked on water and saw Jesus' transfiguration ended up denying Him.

Why? Because emotion is not enough to sustain our devotion.

No matter how many chills we get during a worship service, the reality is that there's a world just outside those doors that is going to pull us toward swerving. And if our faith is built only on emotion, it will fail. Peter experienced this firsthand. Despite his emotional highs with Jesus, he still lost his footing.

We should never mistake what we feel for what is true.

LIE #3: The more I know, the less I will sin.

I know a good bit about diet and exercise.

I know, for example, that it's not a great idea for me to visit an ice cream shop several times a week and attempt to eat my weight in birthday cake ice cream.

I know that the ingredients in ice cream are not what I need to put into my body on a regular basis. And yet even though I know those things, I still find myself picking my route around town according to which ice cream shops I'll have to drive by!

Knowledge does not always equal victory.

One of the things I've noticed about people who have been Christians for a long time is that it's easy to buy into the lie that if we know more information about the Bible and the Christian life, then we won't be tempted or struggle with sin anymore. We believe that our knowledge of Christ will make us immune to sin.

Information does not always equal transformation! We can know what is right and still make the wrong choices.

However, information does not always equal transformation! We can know what is right and still make the wrong choices.

For me, one of the most moving passages in the entire Bible is Matthew 16:13-16:

> When Jesus came to the region of Caesarea Philippi, he asked his disciples, "Who do people say that the Son of Man is?"
>
> "Well," they replied, "some say John the Baptist, some say Elijah, and others say Jeremiah or one of the other prophets."
>
> Then he asked them, "But who do you say I am?"
>
> Simon Peter answered, "You are the Messiah, the Son of the living God."

For once Peter got it right! While the other disciples were sort of kicking the dirt and talking about what other people were saying, Peter came right out and said the truth: "You are the Messiah." He knew the right answer—and yet ten chapters later, he said he didn't even know Jesus.

How does that happen?

If you're married, you will completely track with what I'm about to say. And if you aren't married, I promise that if you get married one day, you'll understand this all too well.

The longer I am married to Lucretia, the more I know and understand about her. I know what makes her laugh. I know what makes her upset. And I know the things I should not say.

And yet, at times, that doesn't stop me from saying those very things.

I recall moments when the words were coming out of my mouth and my mind was screaming, *Noooo!* But that didn't stop me.

The point is, sometimes knowledge just isn't enough.

Now, I am all about followers of Christ obtaining information about Him. I strongly recommend reading and studying the Bible, listening to pastors and speakers in church and via podcast, and diving into books that cause us to explore the deep truths of the Christian faith.

But we need to understand that information about Christ doesn't always lead to intimacy with Him. Peter got the information about Christ right, and yet he still said, "I don't know the man." Peter knew more about Jesus than the most brilliant theologians throughout history, yet his knowledge didn't keep him grounded.

Just because we know the right thing doesn't always mean we do the right thing. We need the help of others to stay on track in our walk with Christ.

LIE #4: I need to make more promises.

Have you ever made a promise to God that at the time seemed sincere and heartfelt, only to forget about or go back on that promise just weeks (or days) later?

I can recall all too well promises I made before I came to

Christ, especially ones about abusing alcohol. On one particular occasion, I remember hugging the toilet and promising God that if He would sober me up and make the rock concert in my head go away, I would never drink again. In fact, I'd become a missionary in the Congo!

Yet just a few short weeks later, I was back to hitting the bottle. Peter, as it turns out, did something very similar:

> On the way, Jesus told them, "Tonight all of you will desert me. For the Scriptures say,
>
> 'God will strike the Shepherd,
> and the sheep of the flock will be scattered.'
>
> But after I have been raised from the dead, I will go ahead of you to Galilee and meet you there."
>
> Peter declared, "Even if everyone else deserts you, I will never desert you."
>
> Jesus replied, "I tell you the truth, Peter—this very night, before the rooster crows, you will deny three times that you even know me."
>
> "No!" Peter insisted. "Even if I have to die with you, I will never deny you!" And all the other disciples vowed the same.
>
> MATTHEW 26:31-35

Peter promised he'd never deny Jesus, even after Jesus plainly told him he would. Despite his bold promise, Peter did just that. Not once, not twice, but three times.

The moment the rooster crowed, Peter learned something we all need to take to heart: promises to Jesus, even sincere ones, are not enough to sustain us in our walk with Him.

I met Christ in 1990, but I didn't break free from my addition to pornography until 1999. I knew all the Bible verses about lust and how I shouldn't be looking at the things I was looking at. I couldn't count the number of times I told Jesus I would never do it again.

And yet this sin kept dominating me and ruling over my life.

Promises to Jesus, even sincere ones, are not enough to sustain us in our walk with Him.

Finally one day I swallowed my pride and confessed my addiction to a friend. It was about 11:30 on a Sunday night, and he and I were standing in a parking lot talking about what was going on in our lives. I was tired of fighting, and I was at the point that I didn't care what he thought about me. I just wanted help.

When I broke this to my friend, he didn't yell at me, judge me, or throw rocks at me. He agreed to come by my side and hold me accountable—and he did! We spoke on the phone every week and he'd ask me the hard questions. Since that night in the parking lot, I have not sought to view pornography.

I had to have help in order to be unleashed in my walk with Christ . . . and so do you!

If we try to do life alone, we'll fail, just as Peter did. It's a spiritual impossibility to become the people Jesus wants us to be without letting others in.

Letting other people in

Scripture makes it clear that it's impossible to maintain a close walk with God if we don't have a close walk with the people of God. But what does it look like to do life with other Christians? How can we avoid the lies of thinking we can do it solo and instead embrace the true community God designed for us?

Look with me at Hebrews 10:24-25 (NIV):

> Let us consider how we may spur one another on toward love and good deeds, not giving up meeting together, as some are in the habit of doing, but encouraging one another—and all the more as you see the Day approaching.

Two truths from this passage stand out to me about the way God designed us to need one another.

First, we need people who are willing to spur us on.

When I think of the word *spur*, I can't help but picture old-school cowboy movies. My dad used to love John Wayne movies, and because he thought they were awesome, I did too. However, one of the things that confused me a little as a kid was why John Wayne always had spurs on his boots.

I remember asking my dad about this one time, and he explained that it wasn't for show—it was to keep a horse in line. If a cowboy felt his animal was acting up or moving too slowly, he simply dug into the horse's sides with his spurs, and the horse would either straighten up or go faster.

I remember thinking about how great it must have been for the cowboy but how horrible for the poor horse. And yet there were times the horse needed to be spurred. Maybe it was wandering off course, or maybe its rider was in danger and needed to pick up the pace. The horse needed a little jolt so it would do what it was supposed to do.

There are times we, as followers of Christ, need to be spurred on as well.

I remember meeting a friend for lunch one time, and during the course of the conversation I started complaining about a woman who had been dressed provocatively at the gym earlier that day.

I said to my friend, "She was straight-up dressed like she was for sale. I was on the treadmill, minding my own business. Then she got on the stair climber right in front of me, and her rear end was hanging halfway out of her tights."

My friend gave me a look. "And how long after she got on the machine in front of you did you stay on the treadmill and look at her?"

Spur! (Ouch.)

I hung my head and admitted that I'd stayed on the treadmill for another thirty minutes.

"I don't think it bothered you as much as you're saying it did," my friend replied. "In fact, I think you rather enjoyed it. If you hadn't wanted to see that, you would have moved."

I didn't like hearing what he was saying. Actually, I didn't really like *him* at the time. However, he was absolutely correct in his assessment, and because he was willing to speak the truth to me in love, it made a difference in my life. The next time I saw that woman in the gym, I moved so she wouldn't be in my line of sight. This decision wasn't because I was so godly but rather because I had someone who was willing to spur me on toward being the person Jesus wants me to be.

All of us need friends like that. Without this kind of support, we will eventually find ourselves in places we shouldn't be, doing things we always swore we'd never do. In other words, we'll end up swerving.

The second thing we learn from the Hebrews passage is that we need people who are willing to encourage us. Every person who has ever walked with Christ has wanted to give up at some point. And if we don't have people to keep us steady and cheer us on, we will end up walking away from Him.

The night Jesus was arrested, Peter made a critical mistake: when he was most in need of encouragement, he went off by himself.

> The people who had arrested Jesus led him to the home of Caiaphas, the high priest, where the teachers of religious law and the elders had gathered. Meanwhile, Peter followed him at a distance and came to the high priest's courtyard. He went in and sat with the guards and waited to see how it would all end.
>
> MATTHEW 26:57-58

Before Peter knew it, he was in an environment where he was actually sitting down with the people who had arrested Jesus—without the support of his friends. If we walk away from the people of God, we'll never be able to stay true to what we believe.

Peter was experiencing a "treadmill moment"—his faith was being rocked, and his commitment to Christ was on the verge of wavering. He needed the support and encouragement of the other disciples more than ever.

As Peter was about to find out, we humans are not strong; we're weak. And in those times when our faith is tested, we desperately need people to come alongside us and let us know they're with us and they're going to walk through the fire right by our side.

My father and I had some good times and some bad times as I was growing up, but I honestly believe he did the best he could in raising me. I deeply loved my dad, and I knew he loved me.

In 2006 the news I'd feared for a year or two became reality: Dad had Alzheimer's disease. If you've never witnessed this disease destroy someone you love, take my word that it's brutal and will leave you looking at the sky, asking God why.

I would take my little girl to visit her grandfather on Saturdays, but he never really knew her name. Dad gradually went downhill, until one awful day when I went to see him, he didn't even know who I was. My own father didn't recognize me. It was a wound I wasn't sure I could survive.

What got me through? It wasn't digging deep and finding my own inner strength. It wasn't emotional worship services. It wasn't head knowledge about the Bible or theological principles. It wasn't my promises to God that I was going to make it.

In those times when our faith is tested, we desperately need people to come alongside us and let us know they're with us and they're going to walk through the fire right by our side.

I made it through because of my friends, who were willing to be "Jesus with skin on" for me. These friends constantly stepped up to help me take care of my father and to encourage me as I watched him decline.

Dad went to be with Jesus on Friday, July 29, 2011. I never will forget receiving the phone call informing me that he'd passed away. After losing my mother nearly thirty years earlier and now losing my father, I felt so lonely—truly like an orphan. I had the overwhelming sensation that no one was left on this planet for me, and the grief threatened to swallow me.

My wife, Lucretia, was a tremendous help to me during that time. She was consistently there for me and asked how she could help. I told her I didn't know—that the best way to describe how I felt was *lonely*.

Lucretia immediately went into action. She contacted some of our close friends, who changed their plans for the evening and arranged to have a huge dinner brought to our house. That night our home was filled with people who loved me and who made it a priority to be there to do life with me. We laughed together and cried just a little, and to my surprise, most of the feelings of loneliness faded away.

When I was weak, my community was strong. I experienced God's unleashing grace in a new way that night in the midst of my grief. I learned firsthand that life is not meant to be lived alone. I needed encouragement, and my friends were there to give it to me when I needed it most.

The enemy doesn't want us in church. He doesn't want us to have deep, meaningful friendships with people who know us and love us anyway. He knows that in order to get to us, he needs to isolate us. As I've seen happen so many times, the first step people take away from God is usually a step away from church and their friends.

Peter couldn't do life alone, and neither can we. If we stay committed to God's church and to one another, there will be times of spurring and times of encouragement. And most of all, we'll experience God's unleashing grace within the context of community.

When we walk with Christ, we do not have to walk alone!

CHAPTER 10

CROSSING THE FINISH LINE

Lucretia and I went on our "dream vacation" to Saint Lucia a few years ago . . . where I experienced one of the worst nightmares of my life.

We both like to hike, and we also enjoy taking on physical challenges, so when we discovered that a tour company was offering a hike to the second tallest point in Saint Lucia near where we were staying, we made plans to dominate the walk to the top.

Our guide was a small young lady who lived at the base of the mountain we were going to climb. When we were introduced to her, she was polite but had few words to say. I must admit that when I get around people who don't talk, I get a little nervous. So I began asking her questions, trying to lighten the mood a bit.

It turns out that was a bad idea!

The brochure that advertised the hike said the trail was "slightly challenging." (I later found out that's like saying that water is sort of wet!) We started our ascent at what I would call a moderate pace. Then I made the mistake of asking our guide the following question: "What's the fastest you've ever made it to the top of the mountain?"

Please understand that when I said this, I had zero intent of trying to break any records. Nor did I want to pick up the pace we'd established. I was simply trying to have a conversation, and I just asked something that popped into my mind.

The guide obviously saw my question as some sort of crack on the pace she'd set, because after responding, she picked up the speed and we took off with a kind of urgency that just shouldn't happen on vacation.

At first I kind of liked the new pace. But it wasn't long before we began climbing straight up, and our fearless guide, who happened to be in excellent shape, didn't slow down one bit. By now we were passing people who had left about thirty minutes ahead of us.

I started to sweat. Just a little at first, but soon I began to feel a trickle down my back. It wasn't long before the sweat had soaked through my shorts and both of my shirts. I'm pretty sure I looked like I'd just gotten out of the shower fully clothed. However, the Jillian Michaels of Saint Lucia never slowed down, so I didn't either.

Then something strange happened: I started getting cold and shaking all over. I thought maybe it would pass, so I just kept going. But that wasn't the case. After several minutes, I must have looked like a guy at a frat party who'd had a rough combination of too much dancing and too many beers, because the guide and Lucretia stopped and asked me if I was okay. I replied, of course, "I'm fine!"

I knew I was in trouble when everything started getting blurry and I began praying that God would either kill me on the spot or send Jesus back to earth right then. My feet felt like cement bricks and my legs were starting to cramp, and all the while the gap between me and our guide, who appeared bent on torturing me, continued to widen.

We finally came to a bench on the trail, and I collapsed onto it, trying to catch my breath. After a while our guide came back to check on us, and I asked her how much farther it was to the top. When she told me we still had about twenty minutes or so to go, I uttered the words I'd been thinking for the past thirty minutes: "I quit!"

I told Lucretia to go to the top without me, that I'd be fine right in the middle of the jungle on that bench. She asked if I was sure, and after I'd assured her I was, she and Ms. Hike-Till-You-Drop took off, leaving me shaking and sweating like crazy.

They came back about forty-five minutes later, and we walked down the mountain to the little base camp at the bottom. When we got there, I mumbled an insincere thank-you and promptly bought every bottle of water the place had.

Later that night, as I was lying in bed trying to fight off leg cramps, I began thinking about my experience on the mountain earlier that day. In a strange way, it reminded me of what I've seen repeatedly in life and in ministry over the past twenty years. Stay with me here. . . .

When people begin their walk with Christ, no one ever intends to quit. I've seen people start off their spiritual journeys with so much passion and enthusiasm that they're practically contagious. But sadly, some people get to a point in their relationship with Christ where they just give up.

Hear me on this. These are good people! With great intentions! Who never thought they would throw in the towel!

But somehow they end up collapsing on a bench somewhere before they reach the top of the mountain. And what's worse, many of them never get back on the path again.

For some reason people have the idea that walking with Christ is a one-shot deal: once you give it a try and fail, you have no hope of ever getting back on track again. *Why would Jesus ever give a quitter another chance?* they wonder.

Maybe you know someone who has quit on Christ in the past, or maybe that person is you. Maybe you've given up believing that your walk with Jesus will ever amount to anything again.

Just because you quit on God doesn't mean that He has quit on you!

As someone who is passionate about Scripture-inspired truth, I want you to know one thing: Just because you quit on God doesn't mean that He has quit on you! I don't care if you quit on Him last week, last year, or decades ago—He hasn't given up on you. He still has a plan for your life. He hasn't forgotten you. And He wants you to get off the bench and get back on the path toward an unleashed life.

So far we've seen example after example of David as a great hero of the faith. That's not his whole life story, however. During one dark season of his life, he essentially quit on God. He turned his back on the Lord and blatantly chose what he wanted over what God wanted. He committed adultery and murder, and then he showed absolutely zero signs of remorse (see 2 Samuel 11).

But God didn't quit on David. Instead He sent the prophet Nathan to confront him and call him on his sin (see 2 Samuel 12). As a result, David repented of what he had done and got back on track in his journey with the Lord. That didn't mean there weren't consequences for his sin; in fact, his sin ended up costing him the life of his own son. But when he showed true repentance (his prayer of confession and repentance in Psalm 51 is breathtaking), God forgave him completely and restored his relationship with Him.

Did you get that? David committed adultery and murder, and still God didn't quit on him!

It wasn't just David either—the Bible is full of people who quit on God but whom God chose to use for His purposes anyway. One example from the New Testament is John Mark.

We first are introduced to him in the book of Acts:

> [Peter] went to the home of Mary, the mother of John Mark, where many were gathered for prayer.
>
> ACTS 12:12

Apparently there was a group of believers that met in John Mark's home in the early days of the church, so he had a front-row seat as Christianity was exploding. Scripture indicates he must have been a key player at this point in the church, because Paul and Barnabas chose him to go on a missionary journey with them.

> When Barnabas and Saul had finished their mission to Jerusalem, they returned, taking John Mark with them.
>
> ACTS 12:25

This had to be one of the most exciting things ever to take place in John Mark's life. No doubt he was full of hopes and dreams about his journey with Christ, and he'd bought in 100 percent to the mission he'd been called to.

However, when John Mark and the rest of the missionary crew landed in Cyprus, they came face-to-face with a disturbing situation:

> Barnabas and Saul were sent out by the Holy Spirit. They went down to the seaport of Seleucia and then sailed for the island of Cyprus. There, in the town of Salamis, they

went to the Jewish synagogues and preached the word of God. John Mark went with them as their assistant.

Afterward they traveled from town to town across the entire island until finally they reached Paphos, where they met a Jewish sorcerer, a false prophet named Bar-Jesus. He had attached himself to the governor, Sergius Paulus, who was an intelligent man. The governor invited Barnabas and Saul to visit him, for he wanted to hear the word of God. But Elymas, the sorcerer (as his name means in Greek), interfered and urged the governor to pay no attention to what Barnabas and Saul said. He was trying to keep the governor from believing.

Saul, also known as Paul, was filled with the Holy Spirit, and he looked the sorcerer in the eye. Then he said, "You son of the devil, full of every sort of deceit and fraud, and enemy of all that is good! Will you never stop perverting the true ways of the Lord? Watch now, for the Lord has laid his hand of punishment upon you, and you will be struck blind. You will not see the sunlight for some time." Instantly mist and darkness came over the man's eyes, and he began groping around begging for someone to take his hand and lead him.

When the governor saw what had happened, he became a believer, for he was astonished at the teaching about the Lord.

ACTS 13:4-12

I've never met a Jewish sorcerer myself, and I've never seen a man struck blind with a simple sentence, but I'd venture to say that was enough to make John Mark want to go home crying to his mama. I don't have hard evidence to back up this theory, but I fully believe this event is what led John Mark to quit.

Maybe John Mark didn't realize just how risky it was going to be to follow Jesus, how unpredictable things were going to be. Maybe this was more than he'd signed up for. So when he began to deal with opposition and uncertainty, it took him off guard and he decided to walk away.

Maybe this event scared him (rightfully so—I can say it would have freaked me out just a little). After such an intense encounter with the supernatural, his fear won out over his desire to be sold out to Christ.

Maybe he was having doubts about this whole following Jesus thing anyway, and this situation was just the tipping point that caused him to throw in the towel on his journey.

We could speculate about all kinds of possibilities, but the main thing to note is that, whatever the reason, he quit.

> Paul and his companions then left Paphos by ship for Pamphylia, landing at the port town of Perga. There John Mark left them and returned to Jerusalem.
>
> ACTS 13:13

John Mark quit and went back home. A journey that most likely began with high hopes and huge dreams ended with John Mark saying, "I just can't do this anymore."

Now this is where things get personal: are you moving closer to God or further away from Him? I'm not talking about feelings here, because all of us at some points will feel as if God is distant. But if we look objectively at our lives, are we becoming more like Christ? Or are we drifting away?

Are you moving closer to God or further away from Him?

We've got to get this question nailed down, because if we are moving away from Him, we may be closer to quitting than we realize.

Based on my observations of Scripture and people, there are four main reasons people tend to quit on their faith.

REASON #1: Misunderstandings

Somewhere along the way a lot of us Christians have bought into the lie that as long as we're following Jesus, nothing bad will ever happen to us. So when tough times hit, we quit—either because we're confused, having never seen this coming, or because we're angry, believing God owes us something after all we've done for Him.

However, when we read the Bible, we see that really bad things happened to people who were trying their best to follow Christ.

We're given countless examples throughout Scripture, but none is quite as striking as the account Paul gives of the way he served Christ and the hardships he faced along the way:

> Are they servants of Christ? I know I sound like a madman, but I have served him far more! I have worked harder, been put in prison more often, been whipped times without number, and faced death again and again. Five different times the Jewish leaders gave me thirty-nine lashes. Three times I was beaten with rods. Once I was stoned. Three times I was shipwrecked. Once I spent a whole night and a day adrift at sea. I have traveled on many long journeys. I have faced danger from rivers and from robbers. I have faced danger from my own people, the Jews, as well as from the Gentiles. I have faced danger in the cities, in the deserts, and on the seas. And I have faced danger from men who claim to be believers but

> are not. I have worked hard and long, enduring many sleepless nights. I have been hungry and thirsty and have often gone without food. I have shivered in the cold, without enough clothing to keep me warm.
>
> Then, besides all this, I have the daily burden of my concern for all the churches.
>
> 2 CORINTHIANS 11:23-28

Um, I'm not trying to downplay anything you might have gone through, but I'd venture to say that most of us haven't had it as bad as Paul.

And to top it off, these things happened to him *because* he was following Christ.

When I was twelve years old, my father bought a brand-new truck. One day not long after he got it, he let me drive it in our backyard. As I was backing up the truck to our porch, where he was going to unload something, I started inching toward a huge cement pole. My dad began yelling, "Whoa, whoa, whoa!"

I've always had a problem with hearing, and I truly thought he was saying, "Go, go, go!" So I punched the gas, slamming into the pole at an accelerated rate of speed. I'm pretty sure my dad invented cuss words in that moment that would have made a sailor blush.

Jesus didn't ask us to pick up our recliner and follow Him. He asked us to pick up our cross.

I learned that day that misunderstandings can be costly.

People have a lot of misunderstandings when it comes to following Christ, as well. Some of us think that being in a relationship with Jesus is going to be easy and that He'll never ask us to do anything too far out of our comfort zones. However, a simple journey through the Scriptures will blow up that theory, as every biblical hero had to overcome at least one incredibly difficult challenge as a result of their faithfulness to God.

Take Abraham, for example. Can you imagine Abraham's face when God appeared to him with this command?

> God said to Abraham, "Your responsibility is to obey the terms of the covenant. You and all your descendants have this continual responsibility. This is the covenant that you and your descendants must keep: Each male among you must be circumcised. You must cut off the flesh of your foreskin as a sign of the covenant between me and you. From generation to generation, every male child must be circumcised on the eighth day after his birth. This applies not only to members of your family but also to the servants born in your household and the foreign-born servants whom you have purchased."
>
> GENESIS 17:9-12

I'm not sure about you, but I would have been asking some serious questions at this point. ("You want me to cut *what*? With *what*?") And I probably would have been asking God for a valid form of identification.

And then there are Jesus' words about the cost of following Him:

> He said to the crowd, "If any of you wants to be my follower, you must turn from your selfish ways, take up your cross daily, and follow me."
>
> LUKE 9:23

As we seek to live an unleashed life, we need to make sure we have an accurate grasp of what it means to follow Christ. If we don't have a true picture of the cost required for being a Christian, we will quit. Jesus didn't ask us to pick up our recliners and follow Him. He asked us to pick up our crosses. And those who won't carry their crosses will always drop out.

Don't misunderstand: following Jesus isn't going to be easy. But it's always worth it.

REASON #2: Difficult circumstances

One year when Lucretia and I were in Panama City Beach, Florida, we decided to take a dolphin tour. The idea was that we would ride WaveRunners to a certain location in the ocean, where dolphins would come up and maybe even get close enough for us to touch. We were both excited because we love WaveRunners, the ocean, and adventure.

Our guide led us into the middle of nowhere and, sure enough, dolphins were everywhere. We were having an absolute blast.

Then the guide suddenly yelled, "Hey, Perry, get over here! Quick!"

I jetted over to him, wondering what was happening. Our guide was pointing into the water, screaming, "Look, look!"

I turned my attention to where he was pointing and saw a gigantic creature underneath me. That's when he said, "That's the biggest shark I've ever seen!"

I just about wet myself!

I remember seeing the movie *Jaws* as a kid and being so freaked out that my parents had to bribe me just to get in the bathtub. I was sure that to the shark I looked like a Chick fil-A nugget.

I told the guide to get me out of there—that I hadn't signed up for the shark tour!

Needless to say, circumstances don't always go as planned—on WaveRunners or in life. Things happen that cause us legitimate fear, worry, and doubt. It's during those times that we have to decide where we'll place our focus. If we look to our circumstances, we'll be completely overwhelmed and give up. However, if we look to Christ, we'll have the courage and strength to overcome what happens to us.

After all, Jesus rose from the dead, which pretty much makes anything else we could face seem fairly simple to overcome.

REASON #3: Bad experiences at church

Something you should know about me is that I love Chick-fil-A.

My family and I eat there at least two or three times a week. (I'm not kidding—and we've actually pushed that number to six or seven a few times.)

The food is always good, they get the order right nearly every time, and their customer service is second to none. The restaurant is always clean, and no matter how long the line is, people are always served as quickly and efficiently as possible.

So imagine my surprise when my wife came home the other day and, as we were catching up on things that had happened while we were apart, told me about a bad experience she'd had at Chick-fil-A.

I was immediately frustrated. (Any husband would be!) Before I knew it, I'd decided, "Well, if that's the way things are going to be, then I guess we won't be going to Chick-fil-A anymore. They've lost my business."

Time out! How *stupid* was that? Let's review:

1) They always provide great food.
2) Their employees are always friendly.
3) Their environment is always clean.
4) My wife's experience was not in line with what typically happens.

And I want to be fair to Lucretia here—she wasn't saying she didn't want to go back, nor was she angry. She was just telling me about her day; I'm the one who became irrational!

Had I lost my mind? I was going to allow one negative experience with one employee to ruin a reputation of excellence that had been consistent for years? (And who knows what was going on in that employee's life—she could have had one of the worst days of her life and was trying her best to hold it together until she could clock out.)

This may sound like a silly example when it comes to fast food, but I think there are a number of people who have done the same thing with the church.

It has become quite fashionable, even in some "Christian" circles, to bash the church for all the dumb things people in it have done over the years.

I know people who have been devoted to a local church for months or even years, attending regularly, serving, connecting with people, and then all of a sudden . . .

- No one called them when they were out for two weeks.
- Someone at church said something hurtful to or about them.
- They didn't like what the preacher said.
- They didn't like what the youth group was doing.

I may as well tell you now: if we stay in a church long enough, we will see hypocrisy. Someone will say or do something that will hurt us. People will make decisions that we don't like. The pastor is going to preach some sermons that make us mad.

Our first step away from God is usually our first step away from the people of God.

When that happens, the enemy is going to try his best to convince us to just walk away. That's because he knows our first step away from God is usually our first step away from the people of God.

I am the first to admit that the church—every church—has made unwise decisions, and it has hurt and disappointed people in the process. But we'd be foolish to allow one negative thing to trump decades of growth and positive impact that have taken place.

Let's take a look at what Scripture says about the church:

- It's still God's plan for reaching out to the broken, the forgotten, and the poor (see Matthew 25:31-45).
- It's still God's plan for making a difference that will be seen for eternity (see Ephesians 3:10).
- It's still God's plan for reaching the world, and nothing will be able to conquer it (see Matthew 16:18).
- It's still the body of Christ (see Ephesians 1:22-23).

The church isn't perfect . . . but neither are you (and neither am I!). So when we're tempted to quit on the church because of something that hurts us or trips us up, we should simply ask, "Is this consistent with this church's character?"

If we stay in a church long enough, we *will* have a bad experience. But we can let that push us closer to Jesus as we recognize that He uses imperfect people as part of His plan. When other people get things wrong, as they inevitably will, we can beg the Lord to teach both us and them how best to deal with the situation, because the church is still God's chosen tool. If we love Christ, we can't quit on His bride.

If we love Christ, we can't quit on His bride.

REASON #4: Love of the created rather than the Creator

Sometimes we quit following Jesus because we want something else more than we want Him.

We want to date someone we know we shouldn't be with, so instead of doing the hard thing, we give up on Christ.

We become so in love with money that we drop out of church and quit on our families to become a slave to a company that will downsize us in a skinny minute when times get hard.

We become so obsessed with having perfect children and giving our kids the American dream that we lose sight of the fact that, first and foremost, our children belong to God.

This is not a new thing. In the book of Romans, Paul talks about how since the beginning of time God has revealed Himself to us through His creation. But with our constant tendency to twist good things, we default to worshiping what God has created rather than the Creator.

> They knew God, but they wouldn't worship him as God or even give him thanks. And they began to think up foolish ideas of what God was like. As a result, their minds became dark and confused. Claiming to be wise, they instead became utter fools. And instead of worshiping the glorious, ever-living God, they worshiped idols made to look like mere people and birds and animals and reptiles.
>
> ROMANS 1:21-23

Whatever our idol is, when we fix our eyes and thoughts on something or someone other than Jesus—when we desire it more than we desire Him—we are coming dangerously close to quitting on Him. Never give up!

A God of second chances

Are you toying with the idea of quitting?

Have you started backing away in your walk with Christ?

Is your spiritual temperature decreasing rather than increasing? If so, it's not too late. God still wants to use you!

Let's get back to the life of John Mark. We see an interesting turn in the story as Paul and Barnabas were preparing for another missionary journey.

> After some time Paul said to Barnabas, "Let's go back and visit each city where we previously preached the word of the Lord, to see how the new believers are doing." Barnabas agreed and wanted to take along John Mark. But Paul disagreed strongly, since John Mark had deserted them in Pamphylia and had not continued with them in their work. Their disagreement was so sharp that they separated. Barnabas took John Mark with him and sailed for Cyprus. Paul chose Silas, and as he left, the believers entrusted him to the Lord's gracious care. Then he traveled throughout Syria and Cilicia, strengthening the churches there.
>
> ACTS 15:36-41

The Bible says that Barnabas wanted to take John Mark with them—yes, *that* John Mark.

John Mark, the quitter.

John Mark, the guy who couldn't take the heat.

John Mark, the guy who gave up when times got tough.

Paul didn't want him to come along, and the argument became so intense that Paul and Barnabas actually parted ways over it. In the rest of the book of Acts, we see very little about the ministry of Barnabas, while Paul's ministry seems to take the limelight.

From a casual glance, we might assume that God doesn't bless quitters.

But let's dig into this story a bit deeper. Somehow (and we

don't know many details) Paul and John Mark (also called Mark) were reconciled. We see proof that they patched things up in Colossians 4:10:

> Aristarchus, who is in prison with me, sends you his greetings, and so does Mark, Barnabas's cousin. As you were instructed before, make Mark welcome if he comes your way.

Then there's this moving verse in 2 Timothy, which most scholars believe was the last letter the apostle Paul wrote. He likely did so knowing that his life could be taken from him at any moment. In the last chapter of the last book Paul wrote, we find these words:

> Only Luke is with me. Bring Mark with you when you come, for he will be helpful to me in my ministry.
>
> 2 TIMOTHY 4:11

Paul, who had once given up on John Mark, wanted him to be with him in his last days. Why? I believe the apostle Paul understood that even though he'd given up on John Mark, God hadn't.

And if that's not enough, consider this. We have four accounts of the life of Jesus: Matthew, Luke, John, and . . . Mark! The Gospel of Mark is named after the man who penned it—Mark, for short. John Mark, the former dropout, the quitter, the one who had at one point turned his back on Christ but ended up following Him with such zeal and passion that he was used by God to write one of the Gospels!

Mark quit on God, but God never quit on him.

He hasn't quit on you, either.

Do you think John Mark ever dreamed he'd be chosen by God to pen one of the accounts of Jesus' life in our Bible today?

Do you think Peter ever imagined he'd be allowed to lead the church after adamantly denying Christ three times?

Do you think David ever thought he'd be known as a man after God's heart after he committed adultery and murder?

Of course not! All of them probably thought it was game over, but God didn't.

Scripture is clear that the same is true of each of us:

> There is no condemnation for those who belong to Christ Jesus.
>
> ROMANS 8:1

Read that again!

> There is no condemnation for those who belong to Christ Jesus.

God will do what He needs to do to correct us and get us back on the right path, but He won't condemn anyone who belongs to Christ.

We serve a God of second chances.

So right now if you feel that quitting is the logical thing to do, the easy thing to do, I want to encourage you that God doesn't want you to quit. I don't care who you are or what you've done—God isn't through with you yet. His unleashing grace can wash over the sins of your past and propel you into the future He has called you to.

After all, He has never given up on you. And He never will!

A FINAL WORD

HOLD ON TO YOUR FORK

If you grew up in the South, you understand that lunch with the extended family on Sunday afternoons is a big deal. My house when I was growing up was no exception.

My mother was an amazing cook, so on Sundays when we got home from church, she would begin to fry chicken and okra, make macaroni and cheese with real butter, slice tomatoes, and make biscuits and gravy from scratch. As she was doing so, members of our family would start arriving one by one.

When it was finally time to eat, we would absolutely throw down. My goal for that time was to hurt myself without actually passing out at the table. When we'd finished devouring our food, we'd put our silverware on our empty plates and sit around the table and talk.

Then it would happen.

My mother would go around the dining room and collect everyone's plate. But when she got to me, she'd bend down and say, "Perry, hold on to your fork!"

Every time she'd utter that sentence, I would just about lose my mind!

You see, my mother was the best dessert maker in the world. I have no idea how she could make such mouthwatering cakes and pies, but she outdid herself every time. So when she said, "Hold on to your fork," I knew she had something in the kitchen that none of us knew about yet—something even more delicious than anything we'd tasted that day. She had put together a treat that would undoubtedly cause a party to take place in our mouths!

"Hold on to your fork" became the words that brought utter delight to my Sunday afternoons. It was her way of telling me that, even though the meal had been amazing, she'd prepared something even more wonderful that was still to come.

I believe that if God had a phrase He wanted to say to us today, it would be, "Hold on to your fork!"

No matter who you are or what situation you find yourself in, God wants good things for you. That's what He wants for all His children. He wants us to experience the life, joy, and peace found in Christ—everything that comes with living an unleashed life. It might not always look the way we want it to look, but because He is both holy and good, we can trust that what He wants for us is always greater than what we want.

I really believe that we haven't seen our best days yet. He has something waiting for us in the kitchen that He hasn't brought out yet.

If you are His child, then there's something He wants you to know: He is able to do far more than you can fathom.

> [God] is able to do immeasurably more than all we ask or imagine, according to his power that is at work within us.
> EPHESIANS 3:20 (NIV)

As you step into an unleashed life, you'd better hold on to your fork. The best is yet to come!

ACKNOWLEDGMENTS

I want to say a huge thank-you to the following people. Without you this book would not have come to be.

Jesus: You knew me, You knew every stupid foolish, stupid, sinful decision I would ever make, and yet You chose to create me, love me, draw me to You, call me, and bless me! I'm in awe of You!

Lucretia: Proverbs 31:10 talks about a wife of "noble character"—I think of you every time I read that verse. You are an amazing woman, and your encouragement and support during this process have made it all possible.

Charisse: I love you—forever and always, no matter what! You are an amazing little girl.

Mom and Dad: You are in heaven together, celebrating and seeing Jesus in ways I can't even imagine. Thank you for the life you gave me and for all you sacrificed for me.

Danny Gray: Thank you for fearlessly preaching the gospel. Jesus drew me to Himself under your leadership, and I am so thankful for you and Mrs. Joyce!

Len Harper: You told me you thought that I had a calling on my life to preach—thank you for believing in me.

Carl and Karen Powell: You took a shot on me and gave me my first job in the ministry. I still feel bad about the food fight I allowed the youth group to have in the graveyard! Thanks for not firing me.

Bill Rigsby: I had the honor of serving with you at North Anderson Baptist Church for more than six years. Thank you for demonstrating amazing patience with me and for allowing Jesus to refine me under your leadership.

Sealy Yates: Thank you for taking a shot on an unproven writer and believing in me when no one else seemed to want to give me a chance.

The team at Tyndale—Ron, Lisa, and Stephanie: All of you have been amazing to work with, and your insight and expertise have made this book something that I'm excited about.

Margie, Allison, Katie and Cristin: I'm blessed to serve Jesus with you!

Shane, Wilson, Moorhead, Michael, Paul, Katie, and Katie: Teamwork makes the dream work! I'm so honored that He put me on a "dream team"!

Suzanne, Joshua, Shane, Lee, Jason, and Amy: This would not have happened without your help!

Steven Furtick: You talked me off the ledge when I didn't think I could write anymore.

Clayton King: You have been one of the most encouraging voices in my car during this process.

Dale Sellers: You asked me, "What would you be willing to attempt for God if you knew you could not fail?"

ABOUT THE AUTHOR

Perry Noble is the founding and senior pastor of NewSpring Church in Anderson, South Carolina. Just twelve years old, the church averages more than eighteen thousand people during weekend services at seven campuses throughout South Carolina. NewSpring currently has campuses in Anderson, Charleston, Columbia, Florence, Greenville, Myrtle Beach, and Spartanburg. At each campus, people experience practical teaching and excellent worship in an exciting atmosphere. Services at NewSpring can be viewed live on the Internet from anywhere in the world.

Perry is a gifted communicator and teacher who has a passion for speaking the truth as plainly as possible so that everyone can understand. God has given him a vision and a passion for helping people meet Jesus, and each week he shares God's Word and its practical applications for people's daily lives.

In addition to teaching at his church, Perry is a nationally known speaker who travels the country to address thousands of people at conferences and events including Catalyst East, Catalyst West, Whiteboard, the Uprising, Orange Conference, Ignite Conference, Radicalis at Saddleback Church, and the Dream Center. Perry also speaks at NewSpring Church's three conferences: Unleash (in

March); the NewSpring Leadership Conference (in September), which together attract more than five thousand church leaders from around the country; and the Gauntlet in Daytona Beach, Florida, a youth conference for NewSpring Church's thriving youth group of more than sixteen hundred students.

Perry can also be found online at Perrynoble.com, where he averages more than one million visits a year, and on Twitter, where he has more than fifty thousand followers.

Perry, his wife, Lucretia, and their daughter, Charisse, live in Anderson, South Carolina.